CW01309772

fabulous
faithful & free

A Transformational Guide to Loving Yourself with Boldness

Juanita R. Ingram, Esq.

WESTBOW
PRESS®
A DIVISION OF THOMAS NELSON
& ZONDERVAN

Copyright © 2018 Juanita R. Ingram, Esq.

All rights reserved. No part of this book may be used or reproduced by any means, graphic, electronic, or mechanical, including photocopying, recording, taping or by any information storage retrieval system without the written permission of the author except in the case of brief quotations embodied in critical articles and reviews.

This book is a work of non-fiction. Unless otherwise noted, the author and the publisher make no explicit guarantees as to the accuracy of the information contained in this book and in some cases, names of people and places have been altered to protect their privacy.

WestBow Press books may be ordered through booksellers or by contacting:

WestBow Press
A Division of Thomas Nelson & Zondervan
1663 Liberty Drive
Bloomington, IN 47403
www.westbowpress.com
1 (866) 928-1240

Because of the dynamic nature of the Internet, any web addresses or links contained in this book may have changed since publication and may no longer be valid. The views expressed in this work are solely those of the author and do not necessarily reflect the views of the publisher, and the publisher hereby disclaims any responsibility for them.

Any people depicted in stock imagery provided by Thinkstock are models, and such images are being used for illustrative purposes only.
Certain stock imagery © Thinkstock.

ISBN: 978-1-9736-1509-5 (sc)
ISBN: 978-1-9736-1510-1 (hc)
ISBN: 978-1-9736-1508-8 (e)

Library of Congress Control Number: 2018900844

Print information available on the last page.

WestBow Press rev. date: 04/06/2018

Dedication

This book is dedicated to my grandmother Mrs. Greather Juanita Tinker. Thank you for always being there for me and for showing me what it means to be Fabulous, Faithful, and Free!

Contents

Introduction xi
Why should you read this book? xi
Pardon My French: Self-Esteem Sucks. xi
What is Fabulous? xiii
Nothing Special. Nothing at All. xiv
From Ordinary to Extraordinary. xiv

Chapter 1: The Power Of The 3 "Ps" – Positivity, Preparation, And Permission 1
Being Fabulous Means Rising Above Mediocrity. 1
Positivity. 3
Preparation. 6
Permission 12
Purpose. 15

Chapter 2: Free! 19
I'm a mess. How can I rise above myself? 19
Letting go of past mistakes. 23
From mess to manifesting goodness. 26

Chapter 3: Finances, Fashion, And Focus – Be Fabulous On Any Budget 30
1. Financial Stability is Self-Care. 30
   Authentic peace is priceless 31
   Invest first in learning 31
2. Don't Compromise Your Future for Today's Look: Pay Yourself First. 32
   Strategies for Savvy Shopping: 33

Chapter 4: Beauty Is Energy, Balance, Radiance, And Polish 36

1. Love The Body You Have 37
   Don't shrink yourself 38
   Exercise for Health and Symmetry. 39
   Transform your flaws with love. 40

2. Celebrate Your Uniqueness. 41
   Less is Not More – Modesty and Class. 42
   Shop for fit, not for size 44
   Take yourself on an adventure of discovery 44

3. Polish Your Look 47
   Function and form - suit your purpose. 47
   Essential Wardrobe Pieces: 48

4. Finish Your Look; You're Worth The Attention 48
   The Top Ten: 50
   Expand Your Options: 51
   Tops: 51
   Bottoms: 52
   Shoes: 52
   Accessories: 52
   Jewelry: 53
   Everything Else: 53

Chapter 5: The Terrible Trend Of Big Butts! 54

1. "But" Is A Verbal Eraser. 54
   "But" Negates Our Value And Uniqueness. 56
   "But" Negates Our Dreams And Experiences. 57

2. Is Your Big "But" Holding You Back? 59
   Insecurity Opens The Door To Manipulation. 59
   Don't Let "But" Erase Your Life. 61

3. The Power Of Your Words. 64
   Find Your Cheering Squad. 64
   Be Someone's Cheering Squad. 67

Chapter 6: What It Takes To Be Fabulously Successful 69

1. Priorities, Goals, Self-management, and Grit. 69
2. Manage Your Time, Manage Yourself: Show Your Future Self Some Love. 70

>   Visualization Sparks Motivation 73
> *3. The Power Of GRIT* *76*
>   You Pull Out Your GRIT.. 77
>   Grace 77
>   Resilience... 79
>   Integrity... 80
>   Tenacity.. 81
>
> **Chapter 7: How To Be Free - The Workbook** **84**
> *How To Use This Planner*... *85*
> *WORKBOOK* *89*
> *READINESS Part 1. Financial Self-Care* *94*
> *READINESS Part 2: My Beauty Adventure*....................... *96*
> *READINESS Part 3. Wardrobe Inventory* *97*
> *READINESS Part 4. Polish Plan* *99*

Introduction

Why should you read this book?

Good question. Maybe you're curious about the title or the picture on the cover. Perhaps you like beauty pageants and think you might get some hair and makeup tips. And if that's all you want out of it, that's all you'll get. Frankly, you'll just be wasting your time. But if you want to get more, then dive in!!

What you get out of this book is the same as you get out of life – it depends on your "WHY." If you've got a little why, you'll make a minimal effort, and get a minimum result. If you have a great big why, you'll take colossal action and get unbelievable results.

Read this book because you want to be fabulous! I won't let you down.

Pardon My French: Self-Esteem Sucks.

There's one thing you should know about me right off. I hate **self**-esteem! If you've got any **self**-esteem right now, I want you to just throw it right out the window.

"Hang on!" I can hear you saying it. "I picked up this book about being fabulous because I want to feel better about myself. I want more self-esteem, better self-esteem, not less! Juanita, you're crazy."

Listen, I want you to feel great about yourself. I already know you're fabulous, and I want you to know it too. But I don't want you to sit around trying to build up your self-esteem when you could have something so much better.

We hear a lot about building up children's self-esteem or helping women gain self-confidence to make positive changes in their lives. What it usually comes down to is affirmation: hearing good things about yourself, or saying them to yourself. The affirmations are lovely. It's an excellent tool in its place. Lord knows I like hearing it! But affirmations alone do not change the way you think about yourself deep down. It doesn't change your choices, and it doesn't change the trajectory of your life. Self-esteem that comes from someone else's affirmation keeps you dependent on other people's opinions. It's shallow because it comes from things other people notice. It can even drive you to unhealthy relationships because it's an emotional vacuum that always needs filling with attention and praise.

I want you to develop something much better: self-worth and self-efficacy. These mindsets free you from other people's opinions and create a deep well of security that can carry you on the long road to success. They are with you on good days and bad because you can cultivate them with deliberate action.

Self-worth understands your identity. You are unique, with gifts and experiences that allow you to do something in the world nobody else can do quite the same way. In my faith, we call it "created in the image of God and created with kingdom purpose." You may call it basic human dignity and the purpose of your existence. Either way, it means that people are precious. They should be treated with love, honor, respect, and kindness. You should be treated with love, honesty, respect, and understanding, not because you did something special or because you're smart or pretty, but because you are a human being. It's just that simple.

You see the difference? Self-worth isn't a feeling – it's a principle. It never changes. You're not ever going to stop being a precious human being because you feel fat, or lost a job, or made a mistake. Self-worth puts you into healthy relationships because you see that other people are precious too, and you treat them with love, respect, and kindness.

Self-efficacy is the confidence that you can do a particular task or learn a specific skill. It knows deep down inside that "yeah, I could do that." The fantastic thing about self-efficacy is that it grows and spreads. You may not have a lot of amazing skills right now, but there is <u>something</u> in life you feel competent and empowered to do. Taking some small step toward the mastery of other skills will further confirm your confidence in your own capability. The more skills you master, the more significant your circle of efficacy gets, and the further you're willing to stretch.

Here's the secret - <u>everything</u> is a skill that can be learned. Effective communication? Skill. Studying? Skill. Interviewing for the job you want? Skill. Public Speaking? Skill. Dressing in a manner that enhances your positive attributes? Skill. You can learn them, and mastering skills makes you believe and have a certain level of faith that you can learn many others as well. Self-efficacy is the "sustainable green energy" of your life because you can't use it up and you can always grow more.

What is Fabulous?

Okay, so what exactly is being Fabulous? It might be a little different for everyone. Here's what it means to me: Fabulous is looking great and feeling great, but it's so much more than that, too. Fabulous means being a woman of substance, accomplishment, character, and integrity. It means having high ideals and following through on them. It means working – working hard – for the betterment of yourself, your family, and your community. It means honoring who you are, getting to know who you are and who you want to become, and loving yourself entirely, and unconditionally, without exception – flaws and all!

To be Fabulous, you must be Faithful to your true self and your highest values. You must know and accept your strengths and your weaknesses. You must choose a path that you're proud to claim, and walk it with daily decisions that follow through on your commitments. It takes a substantial purpose, a growing character, a desire to honor yourself and others, and acquiring something I call **GRIT** (I'll tell you all about that later.)

The journey from *Faithful* to *Fabulous* will also make you *Free* - free of limiting thoughts and fears. Free from dependency upon other people's approval. Free from past mistakes or life obstacles. Free to fulfill your dreams and your full potential, and make a positive impact in the world. Free to enjoy your work, your relationships, and your successes.

Now you may be wondering who I am, and why I'm qualified to tell you anything. Maybe that picture on the cover makes you feel like I don't know anything about your life or where you come from. Let me tell you a little about my life and where I come from. We probably have more in common than you think.

Nothing Special. Nothing at All.

Maybe you think you're nothing special. I once felt that way as well. I'm just a little Southern girl from Tennessee. I was a cross between nerdy and somewhat cool in school – I straddled the fence of either "teenage worlds" or groups. My Coke-bottle glasses were so thick; my nickname was "Focus" in middle school, then "Peppers" in college when my switch to contacts revealed my wide-set eyes that my glasses previously covered. Growing up, some kids at school picked on me for various reasons. I had thick glasses and braces – it wasn't always a pretty picture. Teachers picked on me for the way I behaved (I tended to talk a lot in class at the wrong time). Even some relatives picked on me. When you're surrounded by voices telling you that you don't fit in, that you look or walk or speak "funny," that you aren't special, just ordinary at best – that takes a toll.

I started to believe my big eyes were "funny looking." I believed my body was weird and wrong. I kept my head down, kept my mouth shut, and even dropped out of activities. I liked to avoid the criticism and negative attention. I believed I was nothing special, and when you think and internalize that, it doesn't take much to make you think you are nothing at all.

From Ordinary to Extraordinary.

I was just an ordinary gal from an ordinary town, but I've had some extraordinary things happen in my life. The good thing about being called

"Focus" was that I learned to focus on what I wanted. I knew I could make good grades if I wanted. Eventually, I decided that I really wanted to be an attorney, and when I was in law school, I met a moot court team coach who changed my whole life. She taught me what it meant to dream big. She permitted me to be entirely imperfect and to work at my goals with my full heart because when you have a big dream and pursue it with everything you've got, you win something much bigger and better than a single goal - you become your prize.

I've never forgotten that lesson, and it's the one I want to pass on to you. No matter what your goal may be, go after it wholeheartedly. **You** are the prize. Being the best version of yourself is the reward!

After I became a practicing attorney, I got asked to speak to girl groups in my city, especially in urban schools because some of those young ladies had never seen an African-American female attorney before. This was many years after Claire Huxtable on the Cosby Show, and it would be years yet before Scandal was on TV. These young ladies needed a vision of who they could become.

So I started speaking and mentoring, but I could feel a slight disconnect from my teenage and younger listeners. They were teenagers, and they were interested in young things. They already had plenty of voices in their lives telling them what to be when they grew up. I was just more background noise. How could I inspire them to invest in their inner growth when their whole world was focused on the exterior?

One day I was contemplating how I could get these young ladies' attention, and make them care about what I was saying. Suddenly it hit me, like a voice from beyond: Pageants.

Now, I don't know what your beliefs are, and I'm not going to shove mine down your throat, but I do believe in a personal God, and when He talks to me I listen. That was not an idea I would have ever come up with on my own. I'd never been in a pageant in my life, and I didn't want to. But I couldn't deny that if I showed up to talk about goals and success with a glittery sash and rhinestones on my head, those teenage girls would sit up and listen to anything I had to say. So I entered the "Mrs. Indiana United States" pageant. I didn't care about some judge telling me I was pretty, but I wanted that title to help me get something else. The girls and young women I was meeting needed to hear a message of empowerment and possibility, and if that sparkly crown was going to get through to them, I wanted it. I wanted all of them to know that intelligence is beautiful and to offer them up a balanced vision of success and womanhood.

Believe it or not, I won. I kept on winning. By the time my husband transferred to London for his job, I was competing internationally at the Mrs. World competition in 2011. Eventually, I won the crown at the Ms. World International competition in 2012 and was blessed to represent the UK at the Mrs. Universe 2013 (winning the e-vote contest with over 1million votes and comments of support via social media) and Mrs. International 2014 (placing top 3 as 2nd runner-up in the national competition)! Those experiences opened a lot of doors for me to pursue other interests (like acting and hosting a talk show), but better yet, they grew my understanding of myself and how to relate to other women. Best of all, winning experiences opened the ears and hearts of girls and young women all over the world. After using that platform to meet so many wonderfully talented and unique women all over the world, I continued to step out of my comfort zone. During our four-year stint in London, I couldn't practice law in the traditional way because I was a US licensed attorney and not licensed in the UK.

This fantastic experience not only gave me the opportunity to use and prove my legal and business skills in the form of entrepreneurship and starting a not-for-profit business from scratch, but that experience also afforded me the opportunity to help thousands of women globally. I have walked out living fabulous, faithful, and free! I have rubbed shoulders with some of the world's most successful women, leaders, designers, and philanthropists. I was able to create a platform not only to help women rise, but also celebrate those who have cracked the glass ceiling (i.e., the Power of Women Awards in London in celebration of International Women's Day). I did this by deciding to bloom right where I was planted. I didn't mourn the brief hiatus taken from the traditional practice of law while in

London. Instead, I used the strategic skill sets acquired to pursue a higher purpose and enjoy the season I was in at that moment. I was internally beautiful, bold, and **free**! While others may have seen the move as risky because I was stepping away from the traditional practice of law, I decided that I would make it the opportunity of a lifetime and sow, nurture, and water those other talents that God had poured out into me so long ago.

I reaped a harvest and bloomed right where I was planted. In that timeframe, I was able to birth out seven books, become a signed talent in London, and star in a "British Urban Film Festival" celebrated film, host my web-talk show series produced at Pinewood Studies, and start a non-profit that helped women succeed! No fear, no failure- just **Faith**! And when I moved back to the US and returned to my legal profession, I didn't miss a beat. I created and ran a hugely successful corporate boutique law firm and was so good at my craft that within less than two years I was offered the position of Assistant General Counsel with one of my primary corporate clients. **Fabulous**!!!

Those titles and accomplishments alone don't make me an expert. They have however given me some insights and wisdom that I am often asked to share. If you want to know how to be the best *you* that you can be, how to prepare and follow-through, how to change your life and make amazing things happen for yourself and the people you care about, read this book! I know what I'm talking about and I have the crowns, sparkles, successes, credentials, and experiences to prove it! When **you** are your prize, you cannot fail.

Many look at me and see that I have been blessed with a family that I prioritize, a career full of fulfillment, the opportunity to serve others, and the joy of pursuing my dreams without fear of criticism or failure. I get numerous requests to meet and discuss how I can do all of this and while I would love to pour into everyone individually; coaching is not something that I can currently undertake on an individual basis – so I poured most of my key strategies into this book! So come on. Let me be your coach. Take this journey with me. You can be Fabulous, Faithful, and Free in every way!

1

The Power Of The 3 "Ps" – Positivity, Preparation, And Permission

Being Fabulous Means Rising Above Mediocrity.

So, how do we move from a mindset of self-esteem to building our self-worth and self-efficacy? It takes the three P's: *Positivity, Preparation,* and *Permission*. In law school, I chose my professors carefully. I wanted to do well and get good grades! I cared about that outward affirmation.

Professor Kritchevsky had a reputation as the harshest teacher in the law school. I wouldn't take her class for anything. I lacked the confidence to take that on at the time. But she was also the Moot Court coach, and I knew Moot Court would help me grow as a law student, and it would look great on my résumé. My friend Holly was also signing up with me to try out for the team. As it turned out, we were the team!

Talk about tough! It was more like hazing than legal training. Coach K. was Russian, and she'd bark instructions at us. It felt like being interrogated by the KGB. We'd practice for hours, and if we made a mistake in oral arguments, she'd throw erasers and pieces of wrapped candy at our heads! We hated it. We were terrified. But there was indeed a "method to her madness," and we grew. We became good - really, really good.

In March of 2001, we went to the National Moot Court competition at the World Trade Center in New York. We competed in two rounds, and then we lost. I cried so hard, not because I wanted to win for myself, but because I felt so bad about letting Coach K down.

Coach K didn't say much. She never did. Holly and I were nervous about what would happen. Coach K took us out to a Russian restaurant and passed us shots of vodka. She started talking and my mouth just hung open. I'd never heard her say so much in one sitting, but it was what she said that floored me.

She said winning wasn't what mattered. She looked at us with tears in her eyes and said, "I'm so proud of you guys." She toasted us, "Here's to rising above the mediocrity of life because so many people never even try. It is not about whether you won or lost. You are both better women because of this experience. You are better lawyers because you chose not to just sit in class, but to take on this challenge. You didn't coast. You looked for an opportunity to do something greater and you made the most of it. Trying is more than most people will ever attempt to do."

It changed the way I looked at any challenge and undertaking I ever faced. The reality is, there can only be one winner sometimes. The journey and the growth are the real prizes. That experience made me a better lawyer and a better writer. I got to go and make oral arguments against law students from some of the best law schools in the nation and we did have the audacity to step out of the mediocrity of life.

Always look for opportunities to improve yourself. Pressure and heat create diamonds; the more force, the more brilliant the finished precious stone. I know you might have limitations. We all do. But you can rise above those flaws one notch at a time. Rising above your current level will mean different things to different people. Maybe for you, it's getting an Associate's degree, or overcoming your introversion to do volunteer work for a charity. Whatever it is, rise above the mediocrity of life! No one gets anywhere in this world by simply being content where you are today. Have the boldness to move one step up from where you are today. You can do more. Do the hard thing, and you'll rise! It only takes one step at a time.

Positivity

Before we get to the power of positivity, we have to take a realistic look at the paralyzing power of negativity. When we feel less-than, incapable, and unworthy, we just won't try to rise. Nobody bothers doing things they believe are impossible.

We are all affected by negative experiences or words from the past. A lot of us experience trauma and every single one of us has made mistakes and done things we regret. All those little scars inside affect our thinking and make it hard to see opportunities, or hard to believe we can try something new.

We all have different obstacles that block us from pursuing our dreams. Maybe it's too little money or too many responsibilities. Perhaps it's a health problem that limits our options, or perhaps we spent a lot of time pursuing the wrong things and now it feels too late to go for a new life-changing goal.

Finally, we have to face ourselves - usually, we're our own worst critics! Nobody else can pick at all our failures because we keep so many of them secret. But that critical, fearful voice inside knows all the things we meant to do, all of the ways we fell short, and all of the mean, petty, selfish, cowardly messages that contributed to the reasons that we didn't do better.

Fortunately, we can overcome negativity inside and out. And yes, this is the place where affirmation is a great tool. You can learn to catch yourself in negative thinking and replace each thought with something positive. But saying "I am a precious human being" will only take you so far. You need more than one tool, so here's a whole toolbox of positive thoughts and actions:

1. **You should be intentional about whose influence you allow in your life.**

Surround yourself with people who believe you are more than your past. My nickname growing up was "Focus" because of my thick glasses. Later, when I got contacts, people just started calling me "Peepers." They wouldn't (or maybe just couldn't) see me as anything other than the sweet but funny-looking kid with eyes too big for my face. They wouldn't let me grow up or live anything down. Those kinds of jokes don't feel fun. They sting, and they undermine the way you see yourself. Be polite, but honor your self-worth - you deserve to be treated lovingly, respectfully and kindly! They saw me as smart, but not much else.

2. **Reframe obstacles**.

Do you have an obstacle or a life-paralyzing circumstance? A barrier is a blank wall that stops you from accomplishing your goals. Bang, that's it. No chance. A difficult thing or obstacle is just the fact or challenge that you need to account for in your planning.

For example, my significant eyes and slightly introverted personality were always something I got picked on for. I thought my eyes made me funny-looking and didn't like them. They could have become an obstacle for me. After all, how can a funny-looking girl present herself in a professional context and expect to be taken seriously? How can she enter a beauty pageant? How can she audition to be on TV? Some people that I grew up with saw me as smart, but not much more. They didn't see the "it" factor years to come –some of them still don't! LOL. The reason why? Well quite frankly, part of the reason was that I wasn't trying to be seen. Most introverts are necessarily shy, we are just content being with a select few and love our "me time." Also, part of it is because people are quick to feel threatened by people who can use their left and right brain equally and effectively. Society always wants to put you in a box and needs to label you. Either you are an intellectual or a creative, but rarely are you allowed to be acknowledged as both (although it takes an extremely high level of intelligence to be creative, that's an entirely different conversation). I've never fit into one neat little box, and I am happy about that. I am a "whole-brainer" and proud of it!

You must change your internal narrative and dialog – the messages you say to yourself. You cannot control how others see you, but you certainly can control how you look at and value yourself! As was the case with my eyes, I could have permanently internalized those remarks; instead, I paid closer attention to my eyes. I put more love in that area of weakness and worked with it. I learned all sorts of tricks with makeup and how to wear my hair to make the most of my features. (I can do a mean smoky eye, by the way.) It turns out, large eyes look great in photographs and on TV. That obstacle became a circumstance, and wound up being an asset!

Even as I'm writing this, the Paralympics are on TV. Did you know there's a sport called "goalball?" Blind athletes fling a 3-pound medicine ball across the court and try to score (or keep the other team from scoring) in a net, like a soccer net. How is that possible? The ball is full of bells, and the lines on the court are made of textured tape. They play with sound and touch, and it's incredible. I couldn't catch that ball to save my life, and I can see just fine. Somebody loved sports so much and paid attention to what those active, vision-impaired young people needed, that they created a new way to play. How can love and care turn your obstacle into an opportunity?

3. **Match your goals to your values**.

I guarantee you've made some bad choices in your life. We all have. Those mistakes were based on the knowledge and self-awareness you had at the time, but you can make a 180-degree turnaround today. Instead of pushing those regrets away, take a close look at them. Your feelings of guilt can be a mirror to show you what you value, and what you think is right. Don't meditate on the failure. Meditate on its opposite. That is the person you want to become or the thing you want to achieve. When you are clear about your values, choose goals that align with them. Choose a goal that is noble and worthy, not one which is degrading or compromising of yourself. Commit to your passion in life, and be steadfast and faithful to your undertaking.

4. **Reflect on gratitude**.

In every situation, look for something you could be grateful for, even if you don't feel warm and fuzzy about it at the moment. The more you look for gratitude, the more positive things you will see. Your feelings will follow your thoughts. This advice isn't original - you'll find it everywhere from Buddhism, to the Bible, to Psychology Today. Gratitude makes you a happier, more optimistic person. It prompts you to connect with people and show them appreciation. It even improves your physical health. Take time every day to think about specific things you're grateful for, right now.

I'm not a big boxing fan, but Muhammad Ali was right when he said, "What you're thinking is what you're becoming." Examine your thoughts and attitudes. Could things be the way they are in your life because you are the way you are? Changing one thing – the way you think about yourself and your dreams – could change everything in your life.

Cultivating a positive mindset is the first essential step in rising above your mediocrity. Listen to yourself. If your internal dialog is off, you can change it. It will be uncomfortable, just like when you get braces. They get you aligned a little bit at a time, with each adjustment becoming more awkward or even painful. But when you know your values and are confident you're moving in a positive direction, that discomfort is worth it. Do the hard thing so that you can do great things.

Preparation

Once you've examined your values, created a positive mindset, and found a worthy goal, it's time to manifest that purpose into reality. Exhibiting means to make something physical and tangible, so you're going to have to get off your "tangible asset" and do something about it. You can't have a million dollar goal with a minimum wage work ethic. Whatever comes quickly to you, whatever you know you can do well, and you're comfortable with – that's mediocrity. Even if your comfort zone is somebody else's stretch goal - if it's easy, that's mediocrity for you. Choosing to rise means going out of your comfort zone.

Making your dreams become a reality reflects how much you value yourself. Preparation is where you live out your faithfulness to your positive values and goals. Honor your dreams by committing to work them out.

Hard work doesn't mean flailing around in a panic. You have to prepare to take useful and purposeful action, and preparation is a skill you can master. Proper preparation creates calm and confidence. You know the saying, "Never let them see you sweat?" Preparation gives you that poise and grace.

When my husband and I moved to London, I wasn't practicing law in the UK. I am, after all, a US licensed attorney, and I had no desire to take three additional years getting qualified to practice in the UK. I wanted to use my time and try new things. I figured that season was a gift for me to explore some interests I hadn't had time for before. I had been in some theater productions in my youth and I've always been interested in TV, movies, and theater. I had a feeling I'd probably be a good actress, so I decided to try it.

Now, a lot of people aren't very accepting of a 35-year-old married professional woman launching into a whole new area. I got deluged with negativity from people I knew who predicted failure and asking if I was crazy, or at best delusional. I remember being in the UK and attending a group dinner one night with a bunch of African-American women who were also expats in the UK at that time. A couple of them, one in particular, made it a point to tell me how they couldn't believe that I was doing this. I had just finished filming scenes in my first independent feature film where I played the main character's wife – a very noble and key role. One woman there asked me in a very degrading manner if I had to get an AIDS test when she found out that the role required me to have a closed mouth kiss with the person that played my husband; the other told me that if she were me she would never pursue acting as no man would ever want to see his wife on the scene playing another man's wife. It was as though I had stepped into the twilight zone. First of all, these ladies were acting as if I said I was going to do soft porn for a living! I mean good grief, I was playing someone's wife!

Do you know how many African – American actresses would love to get cast in a prominent lead role who had grace, dignity, and purpose in the character? But these women were so busy projecting their fears onto me that all they could do was make up silly reasons why I should kill my dreams and latch onto their fears. The last time I checked, you can't get AIDS (or HIV) from a closed mouth kiss – so let's all be mindful never to put that lady on the PTA sex education committee LOL! As for the other lady, well let's just say there is nothing sadder than watching a person project their fears onto another after having lived a life of regret. It's sad to watch, and she was putting on a full show of it whether she knew it or not. The very film they made fun of ended up being nominated for a Best Film award at a film festival the following year – and I received a nomination for best actress. My husband was quite proud by the way, as he should be. Don't let others pull your focus and know that you can never be successful if you are sensitive to the unsubstantiated criticism of others.

So despite their discouragement, I retained my firm intention to explore the possibility of acting and give it a chance. I have a lot of respect for acting as a business, craft, and an art form, and I didn't want just to mess around or show up with nothing to offer.

So I went into preparation mode. **Preparation** has certain stages and elements that you have to go through.

1) **Mental**:

Put on your positive mindset with affirmations, self-talk, supportive people, and an attitude of gratitude. Some people stop here. They hope or pray that change will happen in their lives, but don't take any action. It is just step one. If you want a changed life, you have to change your actions.

2) **Consultation**:

Seek out experienced mentors who can advise, train, and assist you. Coaches and teachers have the heart for helping. That's what they're there for! They'll give you a realistic picture of challenges and requirements, assess your skill level, and show you options you didn't know existed. Don't be entitled when asking for help or advice, seek wise counsel and be mindful of the person's time. I still meet with my acting coaches on a regular basis. It has immensely blessed my life!

3) **Planning**:

Do your research. Find out what is required to meet your goal, and make time to do those tasks. What will be expected of you? What kind of time and effort can you expect to invest to get those results?

4) **Skill-building**:

Practice your skills and adjust your habits to improve. A child doesn't learn to walk the first time they stand up. They wobble and fall, cruise on the furniture, and gradually learn to balance and move forward.

5) **Follow-through**.

Big goals take time to accomplish. If you abandon your attempts halfway through, you won't rise above your current level. Keep at it!

When I decided to audition for acting roles, I didn't just show up at an agent or casting director's door and say, "Here I am!" I knew I'd have to bring something to the table to make them believe I could work on a professional level.

I read books, watched videos, took Masters Classes online and in person. I took acting classes in London and America. I did online coaching with established acting teachers in London, Indiana, Georgia, and Los Angeles. My research showed I'd need to prepare a couple of monologues for an audition. I learned how to select an address that showed off my strengths. I learned how to memorize and rehearse. I learned how to develop a character and performance.

I practiced alone. I videotaped myself. I worked in front of a mirror. I performed for my husband, for my coaches, and for friends. When I finally met with a couple of agents and casting directors, I made them cry right there in their office. I ultimately secured a job as a host (or as they say in the UK, a "presenter") for an online chat show, as well as a major lead part in an independent film (the one I mentioned earlier which earned me a Best Actress nomination from the British Urban Film Festival).

That shouldn't have happened. Really! Here I was, a little American woman with a Tennessee accent who hadn't acted since childhood and had not attended traditional drama or film school. I was seen as an intellectual, not a creative. I was a lawyer – not a formally trained actor. Those could have been obstacles holding me back. Instead, they were things that made me unique and a perfect fit for those jobs. When the right opportunity came along, I was there – prepared and ready.

Whatever your goal, it's important to spend time in your planning phase learning your niche or craft. You have to know yourself - your strengths and your weaknesses. You have specific gifts in a particular combination, unlike any other individual in the world. I have no desire at this time to be a classical Shakespearean actress. I also have no desire to practice in the area of criminal law. I know that about myself, and I've learned enough about those areas not to waste my time molding myself into something I'm not or have no desire to pursue at this time. But that's okay! I can do television and film, and I love it! I can do transactional law, and I love it. You should do what you love, even if all the pieces don't fit together in the opinions of others. The point where your profession and passion collide is your calling in life. That's where you will thrive.

Sometimes people hear "you can accomplish anything if you want it badly enough," and walk away thinking that just wanting it - the intensity of that emotion – is going to make things happen in their lives magically. No! You can accomplish anything in life if you want it enough to learn what it takes and do the work.

When I was preparing for the Bar exam, I studied 16 hours a day for three months straight. I passed on my first try, in both Indiana and Tennessee. That's unusual. Most attorneys don't pass until their second or third attempt. I had friends ask me, "Wow! How did you ace it like that? What can I do to get those results?" I told them what I did: 16 hours x 6 days a week x 120 days, equals more than 11,000 hours of studying.

Oh, their faces! "Oh, no," they'd say. "You don't need to do all that. I'm studying eight hours a day, four days a week max." Guess who didn't pass?

One friend had to take the test five times. I guess it took that long for her to finish the studying she needed to do. She told me I was crazy for studying so much and even made fun of how tired I looked during the three months we studied for the bar exam. Yet only one of us is licensed to this day. Don't let other people project their "stuff" on to you! When you know what is right and what works for you, go with it! The truth is, they just didn't want to work that hard. They were not willing to surpass their mediocrity and rise above their current level.

Now, part of knowing yourself is knowing what methods work best for you and removing resistance. I know what study methods work best for me. Think of it as the Williams sisters in tennis: For years, Venus was a media darling, and you never heard much about Serena. Venus was on the highlight reel, and Serena was behind the scenes. You know what Serena was doing all that time? Practicing. And when she broke out – wow! You look at those ladies and see that they've been working on their game since they were seven years old. There's an old saying that overnight success takes 15 years, and it's true. When people are in the public eye or tell their stories, you only see the highlight reel. Behind the scenes is the sweat, and the blisters, and the early mornings; the frustration and setbacks and gutting it out.

But what if you put Monica Seles in training with Venus and Serena, and had her do everything precisely the same way? Would she get the same results? No! She's left-handed. She needs to practice differently. Maybe you are coming at your goal "left-handed" in some way. Perhaps you have responsibilities to take care of a family member. Perhaps you have a full-time job that won't let you work every day on your goal. Maybe you have a health issue that limits your energy or requires a lot of time for medical care. It doesn't mean you can't accomplish your goal. You just have to account for those things and plan accordingly.

This is an area where looking back at those past mistakes can also be helpful. If you see a pattern in your life where you get derailed or let yourself down over the same things, find the weak link and eliminate it, or make a way for it to work. Make a plan that incorporates that weakness, any potential failure points. Maybe your winning strategy won't be 16 x 6 x120, but 5 x 5 x 460. That's okay. Succeeding on a big goal over time, and creating a life of passion and joy, takes perseverance. The more faithful you are to yourself when you plan, the more likely you are to follow through and not become discouraged.

Permission

Little girls are brought up to be polite and respect authority. We asked permission to eat a cookie, or stay up late, or go out with our friends. That's wonderful! Children do need to learn respect and boundaries. But when it comes to being an adult and pursuing your path in life, you have to kiss that little girl goodbye. You can't look to other people for permission to rise; you have to look within. **Give yourself permission to dream big**.

The majority of people never try to rise above their comfort level. Seeing you succeed makes them uncomfortable! Your positivity and progress remind them of the things they want or wish they'd tried, and the fear that holds them back. Fear and regret can prompt people to attack you with negativity. It shows something ugly about them, not about you.

While in London, as I mentioned earlier, I booked a role in a feature film as the lead character's wife. It was an unusual opportunity, especially for an African-American woman. We get placed in so many negative stereotypes. Look at some of the well-respected African-American actresses out there: Halle Berry, Lupita Nyong'o, and Viola Davis. Look at their most famous roles: Crack-addicted mother. Slave. The Help. Those all reflect a piece of reality, but not all of reality!

I was so happy to play this part because the character was an educated, happily married woman. That may not sound exciting to some people, but just to have a positive role felt like a gift to me. But even there, people were trying to take my permission away. Again, while I was filming, a group of older women started picking at me and criticizing. It was what we would call in the urban community, a "whole lot of hatin'." Who did I think I was? How could I kiss someone (closed mouth mind you) who wasn't my husband? Wouldn't this damage my law career?

I could see that they were unhappy with themselves and their own choices, and were taking it out on me. I just had to give myself permission to do something worthwhile and be happy about it. Don't let other people's regrets poison your dream. You can't let what other people say about you impact your commitment to your dreams. Develop a thick skin and give yourself permission to take constructive criticism – but ignore negative comments that are coming from a place of jealousy, messiness, wrong motives, and ignorance.

Give yourself permission to be bigger than one job or one relationship. The world always tries to put us in a box: Artistic. Smart. Nerdy. Athletic. Successful. Wild. Silly. Attractive. Unattractive. Tomboy. Princess. Go-getter. Leader. Follower. Mother. Society wants to limit you to one, or maybe two dimensions if you're lucky. If you're a mom, heaven forbid you work outside the home. If you do work, heaven forbid you do anything but that strict practice of your job. If you're a teacher, you can't be a teacher and a dancer. You can't be a lawyer and an actress.

The reality is that we all have different gifts and talents. We are multidimensional beings, and we have to feed the various parts of ourselves. It's one thing to "think outside the box." I'm telling you, don't live your life in a box! You probably have many different interests. Sometimes they'll support each other, like various creative endeavors, or multiple topics of study or professional specialty. Other times they are separate, and you like it that way. I have a lot of boxes, and stepping out of one is just stepping into the other. A productive, full life is like a Monopoly game. You may have three houses on Boardwalk or two hotels on Indiana Avenue. But your whole life isn't that square on the board. You're the player. We will diversify our finances, but we're afraid to expand our lives.

Give yourself permission to be different, even to be misunderstood. When we feel pressured by other people's opinions, we starve the parts of ourselves that other people won't get. If you've spent your whole life operating in a particular role, you may feel afraid to step out and try something different. What are people going to think? In the beginning, I was so scared to do pageants and writing, and all the things I've been able to do because most people just don't do all those different things. It's strange! But I learned that "unusual" is just a synonym for "unique." **Let it be okay** for people not to understand you. You can't be everyone's cup of tea. But no matter what they think, nothing is worse than living a life of regret. I see so many women, and I've heard so many whispers like, "What is she doing? Isn't that embarrassing! Why would she do that?" You don't want to become one of those nitpickers! If you are actively pursuing your talents and gifts, you won't have time to hate on someone else.

Give yourself permission to let go of people who hurt or minimize you, or with whom you just don't have anything in common. If you're going to cultivate a positive outlook by surrounding yourself with positive people that means letting go of negative people. If you have people in your life who are piling you with negativity or undermining your growth, it's essential to **put emotional distance** between you, so that you can ignore their hurtful words. You might even need to put physical distance between you and spend less time in their company. Maybe you need to cut them off completely. **You have permission** to grow up. I did a friend purge at age 30, at 35, and again at 40. The people who deserve to stay in your life are the ones who "get" you - or accept and encourage you - at every season. Sometimes people unintentionally approach others with so much judgment that they fail to see how toxic they have become. Jealousy can creep in, and they suddenly desire to see you win, but only to a certain extent. Don't let others' limited ability to see all that you are called to be, discourage you. Keep those folks at a distance, if you allow them in your space at all. Love them from a healthy emotional distance and try not to judge them for their limitations as well. Give yourself permission to move past old mistakes and keep those who judge you at a distance. Everyone has a reason for coming into your life; know the reason and don't try to make them operate outside of their capacity.

Give yourself permission to have needs: physical, emotional, and spiritual. Being fabulous and positive does not mean you are Superwoman in a

Fortress of Solitude. You have circumstances to adapt around. You need healthy, loving relationships. You need to eat and sleep and take care of your body, and you need money to live on. You need to feed your soul with fellowship, delight, and meditation on things higher and more significant than yourself and your own life.

Don't feel stupid or ashamed if you need help or better tools, or a particular way of doing things. You have to know and accept who you are at this level before you can rise. Maybe you need a checklist or a script to get through basic routines, so you can keep moving forward. Perhaps you need an accountability partner to keep you on track. Maybe you need a coach or a teacher to guide you. Knowing how to adapt and be your best self is wisdom, not foolishness.

Remember, there are significant things out there that are intended for you. There are accomplishments and rewards meant for you. Don't feel bad about accepting them, pursuing them, and enjoying them.

Purpose

"Joy is the best makeup." - Anne Lamott

I know I said there were 3 P's in this chapter, but when you get positive, come prepared, and give yourself permission, you'll find there's always "Bonus Material!" There's one more P you need to know: **Purpose.** This one is the most important of all because it connects to and drives all the others. Having a purpose in life, and in every goal, will set you apart and give you a healthy perspective on your choices.

I went into pageants, not because I cared anything about being a beauty queen, but with a particular purpose. That title was a tool to maximize my platform as a speaker and motivator, in order for me to live out my purpose of helping young girls and women. As a result, the Mrs. International pageant was one of the most impactful, powerful sisterhood experiences I could imagine. It is a competition full of highly professional, accomplished women. Nearly every contestant there is a doctor or a lawyer - and they are all gorgeous! Some of the contestants had attended six or seven times and never broken into the top 15. Competing alongside those women showed me the difference that a sense of purpose gives to your life.

It was exciting moving up through the competition, but I kept getting called first. Hearing your name called first is a mixed blessing because it means you go early in the next round. It's great to know you're moving up, but you may only have about 6 minutes to do a complete wardrobe change from fitness to an evening gown. It's stressful!

When I heard my name called for the top 15, I ran backstage and found a group of other contestants waiting for me. Bear in mind; there are at least 63 women in this competition, so that's 48 women who would give anything to be in our shoes. This group of 10 women gathered around me and said, "Just stretch your arms out, Juanita." They started undressing me, and I didn't have to move. They changed my outfit, switched my earrings, and fixed my hair. Those doctors and lawyers knelt down and fastened my shoes! I stood there, and those wonderful women dressed me like a doll. My team finished in 15 seconds, and I had time to spare to take selfies with everyone!

The whole time, they were giving me words of encouragement and telling me how happy they were for me! "We're rooting for you. We're cheering for you!" One woman told me with tears in her eyes, "I see myself in you. When I see you out there winning, it's like it's me winning." It was such a beautiful experience of what support looks like. That outpouring of love was better than a crown.

There's an old saying that jealousy is crueler than the grave. Think about that. What could be more ruthless than death itself? Jealousy comes from being empty inside and thinking that you need external things to affirm who you are and why you matter. It makes you attack others with negativity because you can't stand to see anyone else happy when you are so miserable. Jealousy sees anyone else receive love, attention, or rewards and feels robbed. "That should have been mine!" If you find it hard to compliment another woman, you need to do some work on your internal insecurity deep down inside. Jealousy and fabulosity cannot coexist!

These women - all of them champions - were not afraid to invest in each other and me because they knew their purpose in life, and it was bigger than that day and that pageant. They all came that day to win. Nobody goes in a pageant to lose! They were secure in their identity and free to celebrate each other. When your purpose is focused outside of yourself, you aren't driven by insecurity, jealousy, and neediness. You can give and receive support without worrying about whether you're getting your fair share. Having purpose puts you in a mindset of abundance, rather than scarcity. Being fabulous is being strong enough to celebrate other women.

I placed in the Top 3 in this competition. When it came down to crowning the winner, I was so happy for the woman who won. She was terrific, and thoroughly deserved it. I was also happy for myself because they announced that the first photo shoot was scheduled for the same day my UK web talk show with Pinewood Studios started. I'd worked so hard for that job; there was no way I'd miss it! I worked hard for that pageant, and I came that day to win. Nobody goes in a pageant to lose! But we all had lives outside of that runway. We already had crowns inside.

Your purpose will also give you a sense of proportion, helping you choose your goals and the means you take to reach them. When you set a goal and make your plan to prepare, ask yourself: Is this worth doing even if I fail? I've seen young lawyers, for example, set a goal of making partner as fast as possible. They do the work, put in the time, and reach their goal. But they don't always stop to question <u>how</u> they achieve it. The wrong "how" causes broken relationships, ill health, or out-of-control stress that drives unhealthy coping mechanisms. If you win by tearing everything else down around you, is that really winning?

Remember Coach K? She taught us that our personal transformation and our ability to discipline ourselves for success were far more important than winning one particular competition. We thought the purpose of that Moot Court team was our résumés. Later, we were driven by the goal of making

Coach proud and winning her approval. Ultimately the real goal was who we became in achieving it.

So when you're setting your goal and preparing, consider your purpose. If you're doing it right, your purposes will grow as you grow. Be faithful to yourself and who you want to become. Then you'll be full of good things inside that you can give to others.

2

Free!

Failure. It's a loaded topic. We get bogged down in our past, in our mistakes and hurts, and we label ourselves by our failures. Those negative experiences warp and limit our thinking so that we turn an <u>event</u> into our <u>identity</u>.

Sometimes a mistake can be so big and so grave that we feel, "Oh, my goodness, surely this disqualifies me from being useful." Past traumas or regrets can dilute your self-worth. Living in that false identity of failure makes you devalue yourself and think, "I am a mistake. I can't be anything more." Letting go of this thinking isn't easy. It takes opening yourself up to other people's flaws and other people's love. It takes wise and unconditional support. And it takes an ongoing commitment to reshaping your mind with the truth.

The reality is – and I have to remind myself of this often, knowing all the mistakes I've made – that whether it's disappointments, failures, hurts, or just hiccups in the road, even those dark seasons in your life can serve a larger purpose. They qualify you to help someone else. When you look outside to something bigger than yourself, even your mistakes have meaning.

I'm a mess. How can I rise above myself?

You know how when you go to a conference, or a community event, they have those name-tag stickers for you to fill in? "Hello, I'm Juanita."

Now, I could put a fake name on there. I could convince people I was Betty Sue or Barbara. The label I put on myself is how other people respond to me. And if I walked around as Betty Sue all day, I might actually start answering to it! It creates a loop that reinforces itself the longer it goes on. I label myself, other people believe me, and that alters my thinking and my reality.

What labels are you wearing on your shoulder right now? Whether you put them there, or someone else did, what are you carrying around stuck to you? Are they about your passions and goals, or do they say things like Loser, Ugly, Lazy, Stupid, Hot Mess, Airhead, Fat, Unlovable, Slut, Junkie, Criminal?

Pull them off. Pull them all off. Every minute you keep them, you're persuading yourself that you deserve the terrible things that happened, and good things are just a faraway wish. Don't play those mind games on yourself.

Whether it's mistakes you made, or just bad seasons or bad experiences, negative things happen to all of us. A big one for me was getting downsized. It was right after I had my daughter. The head of our department at the time selected me for the first wave of layoffs and told me that he was letting me go because I disappointed him by having a baby. He had hired me as his protégé with this big expectation. I had gotten sick with my pregnancy and had to take off extra time. It was our company's busiest period. I wasn't able to take on as much work, and the department head told me I'd let him down.

Now, that was unfair. It wasn't right because my temporary absence had nothing to do with my ability or my long-term contribution to the company. Ultimately, it wasn't even real. What really happened was the 2008 financial crisis. It was the wrong time to be in the retail business and a terrible time to be in the real estate business. We were in retail real estate. It was the vortex of the worst economic crisis of our generation.

My entire department got laid off. It looked at first like some of us got let go, and others stayed, but ultimately in a 6-month period, there was nobody left standing. Even if I'd worked 24/7 and drafted briefs in the delivery room, that job was over. It had nothing to do with me. My supervisor's story about being disappointed was just a head-game, maybe to keep everyone else in the dark about the real situation. And yes, it was also illegal, but sometimes lawyers make the worst managers.

We're all subject to unfair and unjust circumstances in life. For me, being an African-American woman in a male-dominated, and even white male-dominated profession, I don't get the "living-room factor" or the "locker-room factor." White professional women can remind a leader of somebody in their "living room" - their sister, their mother, their aunt. There's a level of relatability. With other males, even minority males, there's a lot of common ground in guy-code. They can talk sports, or get a beer. I don't fit into either one of those rooms, so it creates this excuse, "I just don't know how to connect with her." They don't see you as being just as human and ordinary as themselves, with lots of familiar ground – the same type of education, the same type of profession, and the same concerns of day-to-day living as anybody in your town. And when people don't see themselves in you, it's easy to do something damaging, and ignore the effect on you.

Guilt and self-doubt flooded my life. I found myself with a Master's degree in business, a Bachelor's degree in accounting with honors, a Juris Doctorate degree. I passed the bar exam the first time around in Tennessee and Indiana, and here I was, unemployed. I questioned my performance: did I try enough? I questioned my choices: should I have waited to start a family until I was further along in my career? I questioned my ability: was I a good attorney? Did I have what it takes?

Add to that all the regular struggles of being a new mom, plus a few extra. My husband was getting an MBA and traveling all the time for work. He was only in town one week a month. I had no family close by. My daughter was born very tiny, and she had colic. I had a rough pregnancy and wasn't entirely recovered myself. I remember before the down-sizing, being up at 2:00 a.m. drafting contracts with one hand and breastfeeding with the other, and just sobbing. It was a dark time.

Other people reinforced the lies I was putting on myself. When you have problems, people look at you differently. They're doing that same speculation: "Maybe it was something she did. Maybe she's just not very good." I thought I had a vast network of contacts, but nobody wanted to call in a favor or get me an interview. I was shunned.

I questioned myself and took on these labels. "Maybe I'm not a good lawyer. I can try to color the situation as being targeted, or I can make excuses about the economy, but maybe I just deserved it." My profession was my identity, and I'd always been successful at it. At the time, of course, I didn't know about the future layoffs. I couldn't see the whole situation, only my circumstances. That blame my boss put on me about being unreliable and letting him down – it felt real. This false information distorted my self-perception. Oh, by the way – that supervisor? After he fired everybody else they laid him off, too. He didn't even see it coming.

Feelings of failure don't just happen at work. Whether you're single or happily married, we've all kissed some frogs waiting for Prince Charming to come along. Unless you're very fortunate, you didn't wind up happily married to the first person you ever dated, and that means you've had your heart broken.

When I was young and single, I spent a lot of time – too much time – in an on-again, off-again relationship with someone who just wasn't a safe person to be vulnerable with. I was very naive and very young, and I had an emptiness in me that longed for kindness and tenderness. But I didn't go to a healthy place for those things. I tried to feel those things with a person, and I chose the person poorly.

I got deceived and poorly treated, but I also made choices that allowed it to continue. I had clues that things were not right, but I didn't follow them. Every couple of years I'd see him again, and try to make it work, and try again. But my heart got broken over and over. Eventually, the relationship ended, and it felt like a death. I was shattered, and I couldn't get over it. I didn't believe I'd ever fall in love again or be happily married someday because I was broken.

Letting go of past mistakes.

Overcoming your history is a process. You have to rip off those false labels and let go of the bad things, but you can't walk around anonymous. You have to fill that blank space with good, healthy things, or those terrible old labels will wind up stuck on you all over again, like gum on your shoe.

The first thing to let go of is unrealistic expectations. You have to realize that everybody makes mistakes. Some people's mistakes you get to see out front, especially in this world of social media and reality TV where everything is on display. In real life, you don't see everybody's private thoughts and memories. You assume that because someone looks happy and prosperous, and isn't airing all their troubles, that they don't have any.

We're looking at the highlights of everyone's life – their "showreel," so to speak. We do not see the bloopers that hit the cutting-room floor. So we think, "Well they're having this opportunity because they're qualified for that wonderful work. I could never do that because no-one's made the mess-ups and the bad decisions that I've made."

Yes, they have. Somebody somewhere has been wronged just like you. Somebody somewhere has screwed up just like you. Nobody gets through this world without scars and blemishes. So reach up and grab that sticker that says, "The Only One." Rip it off and throw it away. It's a lie.

The next thing to let go is negative influences. Some people won't let you forget about your mistakes or bad experiences. Maybe they're giving you guilt and shame, or perhaps they're encouraging you to continue making those same bad decisions! Everybody is not cheering for your happy ending, and you need wisdom about who you listen to and spend time with. Good friends see each other's flaws as well as their strengths. They want to help you do better, but they do it by encouragement, not put-downs. They're respectful and kind. They have a sense of proportion and give you hope. Look for people who magnify your values, not your flaws.

When you're choosing people for your cheering squad, think of them as standing around you in rings, that get bigger and bigger as they move out. The center is you and your own heart. Next is your plus one – maybe your significant other, or one close confidante. Next are only a few people, maybe three or four. The next ring has a few more people, and a few more, and so on. The keys that move people closer to the center are "trust" and "commitment." You can like people in the outer circles, enjoy their company, even love them dearly. But unless they show themselves trustworthy and committed to your good, they don't get that level of intimacy.

You might have a child in your life that you love over the moon, but are you going to let her wear your diamond ring to preschool? No way. You can't trust her with your most precious things because she's not able to take care of them. Same thing with your auntie who tells the grocery clerk that you're on your period, or your brother who just can't stop rehashing the painful thing that happened in high school. You may love them, but they don't belong in your Inner Circle.

I've intentionally decided not to share some of my mistakes in this book. My mistakes are not for everybody's consumption. Facebook is not a diary, and everybody in earshot does not have your best interests at heart. If you tell Inner Circle information to your Outer Circle, they're going to assume that it's public knowledge. They'll feel free to discuss it with their Outer Circle, and before long you've got people you don't even know, knowing all your business!

Often, especially with traumas or damaging choices, you need help to move past them. I'm a big advocate of counseling. It works! You may not feel the need for emotional counseling, but you may need a life coach to help you create a vision and a plan for your future. Get whatever help you need to navigate through life without making the same mistakes over and over. Be proactive! Recognize that if you made this mistake, there might be a reason, and deal with it.

<u>Self-care is not selfish</u>. Getting professional guidance is not a sign of weakness. It's actually a sign of strength to say, "You know what? I want to do better. It is a mistake I don't want to repeat." It takes a strong person to

ask for help: it's no light work to move your ego aside and admit you need it! Having healthy relationships, balancing your life, and making a positive contribution are skills. You can learn them. We're all willing to find a tutor or mentor to get better at school or work, but we won't sit down and figure out how to be better at life. Part of being fabulous is getting legendary coaches and people around you to help you be the best you possibly can.

The third step is to replace those lies that fake identity, with the truth. Mistakes and traumas are events. You are a person. You existed before that incident happened. You had a name and an identity. You will continue to live after you've overcome it. So who are you, here in the middle of your journey? You are a learner. You are someone getting ready to transform.

I want you to take that imaginary name tag, a blank one after all the nasty names are thrown away. Write your name on it. And under that, write "Precious Human Being." I'm going to tell you this until you get sick of hearing it: every human being deserves love, respect, and kindness, including you. It's not a feeling. It's not earned, and it can't be lost. It's a principle. Wear that and see how it changes everything.

Don't get me wrong here. Replacing that label and owning your true identity don't instantly erase all your emotions about the past. Don't just slap a Band-Aid on your feelings and say, "Everything's fine! I'm fabulous!" Make sure you've allowed yourself to mourn what happened, or you'll get stuck there. Fake growth is fragile because you haven't healed.

The stages of grief are denial, anger, bargaining, depression, and acceptance. They don't always happen in order, but they must all happen. Anger and sadness are scary and painful, and it's very tempting to skip over them and force yourself into a mental or logical acceptance that doesn't acknowledge how you feel. Trying to skate through the stages of grief keeps you running around and around the same track, with your raw anger and depression leaking out all over your life. You have to "go there." The only way out is through.

When I was jobless, I didn't wake up every day saying, "I know there's a great purpose in this. I believe my God will work it all out!" I cried. I asked,

"Why me?" I was angry and depressed. I had people say I shouldn't let it get me down, or accuse me of hypocrisy because I claimed to be a person of faith. But it's okay. Don't let people make you feel bad about feeling bad. Find a safe place where you have the freedom to own your emotions.

When my bad-news relationship ended, I couldn't get over it until I allowed myself to cry. It's very tempting to cover up with bravado: "I'm just too much woman for him. He's not worth it. I'm fine." The truth is, losing someone causes grief. Whether it's literal death, or a breakup or divorce, you've lost a person you loved, and you've lost a dream of what that relationship would be like. It's okay not to be okay, and if you never go all the way into your emotions, you'll keep running up to the edge and never get out.

One day I cried for 4 hours straight. That was one of many times, but I finally stepped in and said, "I'm just going to cry, and I'm not going to talk myself out of it. I'm going to sit in my emotions and allow myself to mourn."

It's hard. It's not fun. It's not convenient. I had to get a new set of contacts. My weekly disposables became dailies! It was embarrassing. I felt ashamed that this person made me feel so low. But the reality is that I love truthfully, and there's no shame in that. There's no shame in being hurt when someone else mishandles you.

Be brave! Have the courage to go all the way through. On the other side of expectations, comparisons, criticism, labels, grief, and shame – that's where you find freedom.

From mess to manifesting goodness.

So here you are, as a learner, ready to transform. You have your identity and your cheering squad and your support. You're telling yourself the truth and owning your feelings. Let's look at the big picture. What was the point of everything you went through? Did you live your life through good things and bad, only to throw it all in the trash and become someone else? Absolutely not.

Nothing in nature is wasted. Fallen leaves, dead bugs, even animal manure – it all breaks down and becomes good soil for new life to grow. If you keep working the same ground without adding manure, eventually it gets tapped out and unproductive. Manure is stinky and gross. It's not pleasant, and nobody likes handling it, but it makes the ground alive again. In the same way, there are a lot of things in life that just stink. Nobody wants to deal with them, but sometimes it takes crap to make you fruitful.

When my lousy relationship ended, it forced me to not only deal with the feelings of loss but also with the empty places inside me that led me to unhealthy patterns. It forced me to own my feelings and discover that they wouldn't destroy me. Most importantly, I would not be the person I am today without the growth that came from that experience. It taught me that despite the cruelty of others, I could love myself and give to myself, all the honor, kindness, and reliability that I was looking for in others to provide. I am enough.

Your life journey has brought you to a particular place and particular circumstances, with specific people. These are all opportunities for you to pursue your purpose, even when you can't see the path from here to there.

After my downsizing, it took me 11 months to find another job. I applied every week for a job, sometimes two or three. Altogether, I sent 44 job applications before I got anything. The post I wanted was as a commercial contract attorney with Rolls Royce. I interviewed for it early on but never heard back.

However, there was a reason why I got laid off for that long. I'd always wanted two children, but after my difficult pregnancy with my daughter, we decided not to try again. Well, surprise! During my layoff, I became pregnant with my son. If I hadn't had the time to take care of myself correctly, and the gift of a stress-free environment, I probably wouldn't have made it through the second pregnancy. I had extreme preterm labor issues. I wasn't even allowed to go upstairs or pick up my daughter. I had to take medication daily to keep him from being born prematurely.

One day, seven months after that nearly-forgotten interview, I was hanging out at home in full-on pregnancy glamor mode: walking around in my bathrobe with my stomach so big I couldn't even tie the belt, eating turkey bacon and not caring anymore. The phone rang, and the offer finally came. I started in that dream job at Rolls Royce when my son was six weeks old.

It was a fantastic role that opened a lot of doors for me. The best part was the relationships I formed there, including a woman who's now legal counsel at a different company and at one point in time when I had my law firm, she was one of my most significant clients. If I hadn't been available and looked, that job would not have been there for me.

But it goes deeper than that. The 11 months and 44 job applications that I turned in qualified me. That experience gave me the zeal and passion and deep understanding I needed for my more significant purpose.

You'll recall that our family lived in London for several years. The last two years there, I became the interim CEO and the founder of "Dress for Success Greater London." The "Dress for Success Worldwide" CEO called me for that job because I went on volunteering through my unemployment. She knew my story, and she knew that I had the qualification to talk to those women about not having a job, about getting the confidence to go back out and apply over and over. Being let go from a job does something to your self-efficacy. I have first-hand knowledge.

If you've never walked in those shoes, it's tough to tell someone, "Hang on! Keep the faith. You're going to make it." It's different when you say that and add, "Because I did!" It means more when you can say "Hey, I've got three degrees and I was still jobless for 11 months. It's not you. I know you're going to wake up some days feeling worthless because I did too. But here's my story on the other side." Without that experience I wouldn't be able to share that commonality, to know exactly how it feels. I can be a living testimony that the right door will open at the right time, and encourage them to hold on to their feelings of self-worth by going out and giving to others.

All those negative labels I wore – unreliable, unproductive, unqualified – turned into the opposite. I wasn't Juanita, the down-sized lawyer. I was Juanita, uniquely qualified to be the founder, international CEO and Chairman of Trustees of one of the largest women's support organizations in the world. I was uniquely qualified to be there for other struggling women and to produce a chain reaction of giving and manifesting goodness into the world.

Dwight L. Moody said, "Character is what you are in the dark." There's a lot of truth in that. Who are you when nobody's looking? When nobody's criticizing, and there's nobody to show off for? But look closely. It doesn't say, "what you did a year ago, or last week." It doesn't say, "What you could have done, or should have done." It's what you are right now at this moment. So right now, today, with nobody looking – what kind of character are you going to choose?

Are you the person who's still controlled by those who hurt you? Do you choose to stay enmeshed in wrong choices and limited thoughts? Will you double-down on mistakes by refusing to learn from them?

No. As your coach, I tell you, no. Be more than that. Be better than that. Turn your gaze outward and upward to find the more significant meaning of your experience and help others. Start being fabulous, right now.

3

Finances, Fashion, And Focus – Be Fabulous On Any Budget

Now that we've worked on your inner self with faithfulness and freedom, it's time to start letting your fabulosity show on the outside!

As women, we get a lot of mixed messages about beauty and fashion. On the one hand, the media gives us enormous pressure to look perfect, be sexy, and spend money we don't have. On the other hand, spending time, energy and money on your looks is sometimes called vain, shallow, or (especially in higher education) un-feminist. Like anything else, it comes down to your motivation and your attitude.

It's true that an obsession with hair, clothes, and makeup can steal time and money away from your education, career, and true purpose in life (even if your career is in the fashion industry!). Alternatively, a sloppy or neglectful attitude to your physical appearance can undermine your health, affect how people respond to you, and limit your career options or influence.

Balanced, focused beauty is about taking good care of yourself, celebrating your uniqueness, and being prepared to pursue your purpose every day.

1. Financial Stability is Self-Care

You know how cheap costume jewelry can be so shiny on the outside? It looks great – until it gets a chip or a scratch. Then everybody can see that it's just painted plastic. It has no intrinsic value. Once that surface is broken, you might as well throw it away. If you've read this far, you're starting to get the idea that I don't just want you to slap on a fake attitude and tell yourself you're awesome. I want your fabulosity to be authentic – pure gold all the way down.

Authentic peace is priceless

There is no way to walk through your day with real confidence if you're anxious about money. Before you commit to overhauling your wardrobe or makeup, overhaul your financial foundation. Fashion and fitness are huge industries, and they survive by enticing people to spend money – lots of it. I've got no problem with that! Expert help and lovely, well-made things are worth the price. But it's crucial that you know your budget and discipline yourself to stick to it.

If you're in debt or overdrawn, or if you're in denial and just trying not to think about it, you're carrying that anxiety around with you all the time. You may not even feel it anymore, but it's a subconscious weight on your shoulders that is going to undermine your confidence. You know that saying, "Desperation stinks?" Your precarious finances are going to follow you around like a bad smell. People will sense that you're faking your confidence, even if they don't know why.

Invest first in learning

Maybe you're not in credit-card debt, but you're struggling with student loans. Perhaps you're just starting out in the world and haven't landed the job you want. Or maybe your vocation just doesn't pay much – there is a lot of valuable work in the world that doesn't get rewarded in money. No matter your situation, every woman who wants to be successful in the long-term needs to understand her finances and develop the skills to manage them wisely.

The best book I've ever read on that subject is <u>Smart Women Finish Rich</u> by David Bach. The thing I appreciate most about this book is its emphasis on aligning your money with your values. Finances should never be a stumbling block to your dreams or your purpose in the world.

Another fantastic resource for learning the day-to-day details of budgeting and money management, with support for getting out of debt and planning long-term, is Dave Ramsey's <u>Complete Guide to Money and Total Money Makeover</u>. There are lots of articles, tools, and encouragement at his website, DaveRamsey.com. You can also stream his radio show for daily motivation and in-depth advice.

Whatever book or course you choose, seek out learning that focuses on a woman's perspective and experiences. We have situations, expectations, and challenges that are different from men's. You're not going to follow anybody's advice if you're always thinking, "Well, my situation is different," or "That doesn't apply to me." We tend to have problems with emotional spending. We're also tempted to give and care for others, beyond what is appropriate or reasonable. Your concerns and challenges are not generic, so look for specific advice that meets your situation and your particular struggles.

2. Don't Compromise Your Future for Today's Look: Pay Yourself First.

We always need to be reminded of this principle. Sometimes people will use this saying to justify splurging on a luxury item that's beyond their means. But that's not the point. Paying yourself first means saving for the future and investing in assets that will grow, not indulging short-term desires. No matter how much you love that designer dress, it is not an "investment piece." The minute you walk out of the store, it's just secondhand clothes.

Don't get me wrong: I have a nasty little shoe habit, and I have for years. At 5'4", I love high heels. Even when they're torture, I love them. I must have 80 pairs of designer heels – I was wearing Christian Louboutin and Jimmy Choo long before "Sex, and the City" was even on T.V. But I've never put a single pair on a credit card. I pay cash, and almost never pay retail – I'll tell you how a little later on.

If you're buying a $5,000 outfit and you don't have $5,000 in savings – that is not fabulous. That's foolishness, and it's high time someone called that out. Especially for young women in your twenties and early thirties, I think it's easy to fall into that trap because you feel invincible or that the future is a long way away. But part of being fabulous is being prepared, and part of being prepared is being financially savvy. I've had plenty of friends wind up digging out of debt for years, with nothing to show for it but a closet full of beautiful, worthless pieces of fabric. Do you really want to be 30, 35, or 40, not owning a home, not owning your car, but wearing a $1,200 pair of shoes that you put on a credit card? Don't be that girl. No dress or pair of shoes is worth your peace of mind.

Dressing within your means takes courage and savvy. Courage, because sometimes it's hard to break away from all those messages that "only the best will do" and "you deserve some luxury." You do deserve to look and feel your best, but that's not about how much money you spend or the name on the label. I have a pair of Chanel shoes that feel like walking on a cloud. They're lovely, but wearing Chanel doesn't make me important, or better than anyone else.

Look at our former First Lady, Michelle Obama. Look at her. Have you ever seen her looking less than fantastic and perfectly put together? Well, she shops at Target. She's known for wearing clothes from J. Crew, Gap, H&M and ASOS – and shopping on sale. She doesn't need a label to make her important – in fact; she's put up-and-coming designers on the map by wearing their work. You don't need a tag, either. You're important because of who you are and what you're here to do.

Strategies for Savvy Shopping:

You can make an outfit from Wal-Mart look like a million dollars if you know what works for you and how to finish it off with the right touches. Back in 2009, I did a national competition called Mrs. U.S. Beauty. It was at the time when I just got downsized, but I'd already signed up. I knew I had to do the competition on a tight budget. I was not going to spend $2,000 on a gown or $1,000 on an opening number outfit. I paid $250 for my gown and beaded it myself. I spent about $150 on my opening number outfit. For another category, I wore a suit I already owned and just added some pearls and rhinestones around the collar, but that suit fit me perfectly. I won in every single category. It's all about presentation, radiating confidence, and of course, having a good tailor.

The first step in building a savvy fabulous wardrobe is knowing what works for you, so you don't waste money on the wrong items. In part II of this chapter, we'll learn how to apply style principles to your unique look. In part III, we'll go over the essential building blocks of a flexible wardrobe.

Good tailoring is labor-intensive, while simple blocky shapes are easy to mass-produce. Subconsciously, we all know that without thinking about it, so clothes that fit perfectly look expensive. You can make off-the-rack or even discount clothes look designer by buying slightly larger than your largest part and having them tailored. I always purchase evening gowns two sizes too big for that very reason. You can find tailoring services at department stores, many dry cleaners, and on Google. The result will look like you spent far more on the garment than you actually did, even with the tailor's fee included.

Accessories are another great way to make affordable pieces look luxurious. For example, I went to a runway show during London Fashion Week Festival, and there was just an abundance of brooches. I mean stacking them, wearing clusters of brooches, brooches everywhere. Well, you don't have to break the bank and change your entire wardrobe to incorporate a brooch. I have some pieces and accessories that cost me all of six dollars, and I regularly hear, "Where did you get that?" The right pieces truly make me feel like a million dollars, no matter what they cost.

I'm a big proponent of consignment shopping and estate sale shopping. I've gotten some of the most brilliant timeless pieces, like vintage Chanel from estate sales. There are even eBay estate sale stores that specialize in luxury items, and you won't believe how affordable they can be.

There are also designer consignment stores where they sell clothes and shoes that have been used on the runway or have been sitting on display. They can be 80% off. You can research places like this near you, or that you can shop online. Then take your savings and invest it for your future.

Some people are squeamish about clothes that have been on someone else's body. But let's face it: Shoes and the clothing that you buy in the store were tried on by somebody else, so get over it.

Okay, I know that a tried-on shoe and vintage or secondhand garments are two different things. I get that. But if you're not willing to get creative with your shopping, then you need to stay in your economic lane. Buying on consignment can bring a different level of couture within reach of a modest budget, but it's not for everybody, and that's okay. You can buy retail and discount and make the most of it, but stay within your means.

Part of what you need to do as a real savvy fab girl is learning different options for whatever economic level you're living in. For some, a $2,000 shoe might be the same as a $200 shoe or a $20 shoe to someone else. Building your fabulosity should be something you do sensibly. Make wise choices that are financially comfortable, and make sure that you have the other components of your financial house in order. There's nothing worse than a woman stepping out looking like a million bucks, but her net worth is $20. That's just feeding a false image, that doesn't reflect who you are and who you hopefully strive to be. So don't be afraid to exercise your savvy and build a wardrobe that supports your dreams instead of mortgaging them.

4

Beauty Is Energy, Balance, Radiance, And Polish

We are more than just our bodies, but we do live in our bodies. They are our home and our way of experiencing and expressing ourselves in the world. You can't neglect the inner or the outer self if you want to be healthy and happy. Spending a little time every day on your appearance sends a very real message to yourself and other people: You think well of yourself. You're worthy of the attention, honor, and care. You have something to say that's worth hearing and something to do that's worth doing right.

One big misconception about pageantry is that you're competing against the other girls. In reality, the contestants are apples and oranges. There is no single objective standard of which contestant is "most beautiful," regarding things you can measure. How could I, at 5'4" with a body that's borne two children, compete objectively against a 6-foot-tall blue-eyed blonde who's a professional model? I can't strive to be like her – it's physically impossible. If we wore the same gown – even if I put on platforms and bleached my hair, we will be entirely different. And you know what? I've beaten girls like that on the pageant stage on numerous occasions.

The only competition that matters is you, working to be your best. It doesn't matter if you are 5'5" or 6'5", you can keep on being the best you. That's all that matters.

1. Love The Body You Have

There are aesthetic principles of fashion, fitness, hair, and makeup. Learning to use these laws are going to transform the way you look and feel, but they are going to look different for each person. You need to develop an understanding of Line, Ratio, Symmetry, and Color, and learn to apply them to your own body and lifestyle. You must learn what works for you!

The line is a visual expression of your presence and energy. If you've ever danced, played sports, played an instrument, or sing, you already know how important good form and follow-through are in your movements. Properly aligned posture and relaxed, natural movement improve your breathing, your voice, your stamina, and accuracy. When people talk about "projecting your energy" or "charisma," it's not some woo-woo magic visualization. It's a free, well-supported flow of speech and movement, and anything that breaks that flow is going to diminish your presence. Mental and emotional factors like anxiety, lack of preparation, confusion, or bad habits like poor posture will make your body tense up and break the flow.

The lines of your clothes can also visually enhance or undermine your energy flow. Clothes that pinch, pucker, gap, ride up or hit you at the wrong level will cut off your visual line (besides being uncomfortable!) This is why you see fashion advice like "match your shoes to your legwear to look taller." Taller isn't necessarily better, but you are extending your line to extend your presence.

Ratio is a fascinating subject that could be a whole book on its own. (In fact, there are thousands out there!) Our brains are hard-wired to love a proportion of two-thirds to one-third. This relationship is called the "Golden Ratio" or the "Divine Proportion." Mathematically, it's shown as 1.618. It sounds odd, I know, but this proportion is everywhere. The features of your face are grouped this way. So are your joints in proportion to your height. This number shows up in the placement of flower petals and the spiral of the galaxies. Artists and designers use it because when we see it, our brains automatically say, "Beautiful!" The Eiffel Tower, the

Mona Lisa, and even the iPhone are designed around it. Using the Golden Ratio in outfits makes them look "right."

Symmetry is when you are balanced on both sides - top and bottom, front and back, left and right. In fashion, this doesn't always mean matching, but you do need an "equal and opposite" force. For example, women with generous hips usually look well in wide-neck or off-the-shoulder tops, because it balances them top and bottom. Gals with an "edgy" look often balance an asymmetric haircut with a statement earring (or multiple piercings) on the shorter side. Ladies with a full bust can pull off peplum jackets when the rest of us can't because it balances them front and back.

Color is the key to your radiance. Every color isn't for everybody, but nearly every color has some shade that will work for you. You'll find all sorts of systems out there for analyzing which colors suit you, but once you find your palette, stick with it. One place to start is thinking about people's reactions to you when you wear certain outfits. Color affects us subconsciously, and people don't always realize it's the color they're responding to. Do you have an outfit that consistently gets compliments like "You look so fired up today," or "You look so refreshed, have you been on vacation?" Or perhaps you're annoyed by people always asking if you feel okay when you're perfectly fine. You've just started your list of which colors to wear more of and which ones to throw out!

Don't shrink yourself

Body size and body shape are hot-button issues for just about all of us. All of our lives we get messages from family, authority figures, peers and culture that we need to take up less space. It's good to be healthy, and there's no question that the modern American lifestyle has too much fatty food and not enough exercise in it. But there's also a strong and dangerous link between wanting to be "good enough" and wanting to be "skinny enough."

I know beauty pageants sometimes can reinforce a false idea of physical perfection. But the "ideal" of beauty changes over time and in different cultures. In traditional cultures where you didn't have food around you all day long, being larger was a sign of prosperity and fertility. Today, being slim is associated with self-discipline and achievement, and plus-size women are stigmatized as "not caring" about their health or appearance. Both extremes are false. You can't listen to culture or media for your self-definition because you will always be flooded with two conflicting messages: "You are not enough," and "You are too much." It will make you crazy.

The craziness comes in criticism of our bodies: too short or too tall, too petite or too large. It begins with our expression: too shy or too loud. It starts in our minds: too dumb or too smart. It takes root in our dreams and ambitions: too dull or too unrealistic. This treadmill will never stop, and you can't possibly keep up. You have to jump off. I'm right here. Jump!

Don't shrink yourself. You have a place in this world and a reason to be here. Not everybody will understand your mission in life. They don't have to. When you start working on being your best self and getting the skills to look and feel fabulous, some people will think you're too much. You may have been the ugly duckling who couldn't match her socks, but you are entitled to a new season in life. Those who get it will get the best of you, and those who don't will get less of you. So be it.

Exercise for Health and Symmetry.

Energy and balance also come from functional fitness and health routines. Just like with Preparation in Chapter 1, and Letting Go in Chapter 2, I can't emphasize enough the importance of expert advice. Health issues should be discussed with your doctor and possibly a nutritionist. For fitness, nothing can replace the help of a good trainer.

Even if you can only afford one session, or a group class with a Groupon, or a barter arrangement with someone you know, consult a certified trainer. It's the quickest way to get on the right track toward expressing your physical potential. A coach or trainer who specializes in fitness competition can give you the insight about symmetry and help you set realistic personal goals.

The coach I worked with for my pageants blew my mind when he explained that looking your best isn't about having a specific measurement of your body. It's about what is symmetrical for you. He told me, "There's no point in you trying to aspire to have a 26-inch waist. That is not going to make you your most symmetrical." Without his perspective, I could have knocked myself out working for a goal that was not just unrealistic, but counterproductive. A fitness competition trainer can give you your optimal symmetry measurements, which may not be as small as you think. It depends on the width of your shoulder, your height, your hips, and legs – it's all about balance and proportion.

We strive for a certain number on the scale or a certain jeans size, but you're going to look and project better if you know what makes you symmetrical. I stopped looking at the scale. The trainer I work with now won't allow me to! It's not about a number, but how I feel in my clothes and out of them. Every time you pick up a magazine or watch TV, you'll get pressured to lose "that pesky 10 pounds." It's not about any pounds. It's about your uniqueness and how you can be your absolute best.

Transform your flaws with love.

What do you think when you look in the mirror? There's nothing wrong with seeing something that you don't necessarily like. We all have things we wish we could change. Whether we feel like our nose is the wrong shape or our calves are too big, we are our worst critic. The way you deal with that is to make sure that you love to those parts of you. Learn to cater to those areas and speak to that area lovingly.

You know I got teased growing up for having big eyes. I finally said to myself, "You know, stop saying I have big eyes. My eyes are **bright**. My eyes are **energetic**." I'll never forget the first boy who told me back in high school that my eyes were beautiful. I was taken aback. I couldn't believe he was serious. But when I started saying it to myself, eventually over time, my eyes became my favorite feature. I invested time and energy learning how to make the most of them, but if I hadn't reshaped how I described them to myself, I don't know if I would have been able to embrace that part of my body as well as I do now.

Whatever you perceive as a flaw, give that area extra love and attention. Change the way you speak about it. Love is what transforms weakness into a strength. Everybody's going to have an opinion about you, but what matters the most is your opinion about yourself. Make it a good one!

2. Celebrate Your Uniqueness.

It's great to stay current on trends, but not to be a slave to them. If you develop an awareness of trends, you can fit them into your wardrobe sensibly and realistically - knowing what looks good on you, and what you can comfortably afford. It's about growing and being brave enough to say, "You know what? I know jumpsuits are in, but I don't like jumpsuits." You'd be surprised how many people will give in and spend money on something they don't even like, or they may be like my friend who's six feet tall. A jumpsuit frankly makes her look ridiculous.

We all want to feel accepted, connected, and like we belong. Sometimes that desire can lead us to follow the crowd and just do what's popular, whether or not it's right for us. Trial-and-error is a natural part of the maturation process, and we all go through it. But understand that nobody can give you true validation unless you're true to yourself.

When we are trying to be what other people want us to be, we're operating outside of our true identity and purpose. Even if we get approval, it doesn't stick because we know it's false. You're always going to lean toward your authentic self, and until you are walking in that deep down inside, you can't feel really validated for who you are.

When I was 14, I was completely flat-chested and very insecure about it. I mean, everybody else was developing, and I had nothing there. I started stuffing my bra. The problem was, that made me even more nervous and insecure because I lived in fear that people would find out! I walked around terrified that my "little helpers" were going to fall out. "Oh my goodness, it's time for the gym? I don't want to run right now!"

The worst part was, I committed to the lie and then had to keep it up. I mean, when you're 14 and a B-cup one day, if you show up the next morning deflated, that's even worse. I knew I was lying to everyone just by walking around looking like that, and I was afraid and embarrassed all the time. I wasn't being authentic, and I shrank myself.

If you're making choices about work or relationships or your body, or even fashion because your parents or your peers or the universal "they" say you should, you're not authentic. You shrink your options. You shrink yourself. But when you live out your uniqueness, you can love what you do every day. You feel secure in knowing who you are.

Less is Not More – Modesty and Class.

Looking great isn't about how much skin you show. It's about the line, color, symmetry, and ratio. Wearing a cut-out backless dress may be trendy, but it may also cut your line at the worst possible place and make you look shorter or lumpier than you are! We lose class as we lose material. The Kardashian/Black Chyna/ Amber Rose culture dictates that you must show an abundance of skin to be fabulous, but that's so wrong. The reality is that a classy outfit will always showcase you better than a trashy outfit.

Even if you think the actresses and models in magazines look fantastic, remember that those images are often altered and not real. You could run out and buy the same outfit some celebrity is wearing, but unless you've spent the tens of thousands of dollars that some of them have on surgically enhanced bodies, and have a team of professional stylists following you around, you're not going to look the same. It's even been rumored that Janet Jackson had a rib removed to reshape her torso. Other actresses have fat sucked out of the normal places and injected into others. And on top of that, the images themselves are touched up, and parts of their body get painted out. Photos and even videos can be altered, but you can't Photoshop real life.

I'm not trying to be harsh, and I'm not trying to be mean. I'm trying to be realistic. When you squeeze yourself into a skin-tight, barely-there outfit, you do not look how you think you do. Even if you try on everything in a three-way mirror, you cannot see yourself from all angles, and I guarantee that your reality is sticking out somewhere. You won't see it, but the rest of the world will, and you will not be making the impression you intended. I want you to present yourself in the best light. It doesn't mean that you have to wear turtlenecks all the time, but your clothes need enough space and coverage to create flattering lines in 360 degrees.

As an intelligent woman, you're capable of making smart decisions. Understanding how you look to others shows self-awareness and self-possession. Being smart is fabulous, and you can be fabulous without showing every bit 'and piece of your body.

My very first pageant was "Mrs. Indiana United States," and won every category, including swimsuit. Most of the other contestants wore two-pieces (even the ones who maybe should not have.) I was so modest about walking the stage in my swimsuit, I had on a full one-piece, with nylons and a wrap skirt. That thing was a dress by the time I was done with it.

I could have pulled off a two-piece at that stage in my life before I had kids and I wear them now at the beach all the time. But because I was doing pageants to enhance my credibility and ability to speak to and motivate young women, it was necessary for me to prove a point. I wanted to show that you can be gorgeous and successful without compromising your boundaries. We were on a stage; we were not at the beach. I wanted to stand up on stage in something I could wear in front of anyone I respected, without feeling embarrassed or ashamed.

That's a good rule of thumb, actually. No matter where you're going, you should be dressed as if you'd be seen by someone you respect and hold in high esteem. It's true because the person you should respect the most is yourself. Are you doing yourself justice? Are you making yourself proud?

Shop for fit, not for size

A great fit is not about the number on the label. It's about knowing what works on your body frame. The number on the tag is meaningless, truly, and the sooner you absorb that, the happier you'll be. I'm 5'4", and I vary from a size 2 to a size 8 without gaining a pound! It all depends on what store you're in, who the designer is, where the clothes were made, and how they're constructed.

Cultivate the mindset that you are the judge of the clothes, not the other way around. That garment has a job - to make you look and feel great. You know that Facebook meme - "You had one job!" If that dress or those pants aren't doing their job, they failed, not you. Never let a piece of cloth tell you how to feel about yourself.

Take yourself on an adventure of discovery

The most important lesson I learned about fashion and fabulosity was from a pageant coach named Lisa. She taught me that finding your look is part of coming into an awareness of yourself. Everything is not meant for everybody, and just because a particular color or cut is in style doesn't mean you should pick it up. Sometimes you can take trends and adapt them to suit you, but you need to know yourself inside and out.

You need to know your body, your skin tone, and your lifestyle and understand how all those things work together. You need to take yourself on a journey and discover who you are and what is best for you.

Now, you know what I'm going to recommend, right? **Expert advice**.

You can start off with some resources to learn about the principles of style. For a better understanding of line, ratio, and symmetry I recommend the "Inside Out Style Blog" at insideoutstyleblog.com. There are articles and great visuals there that can show you how the Golden Ratio works for pairing outfits, for example, or how to choose the right hem length for your legs and height. I also recommend "What You Wear Can Change Your Life" by Trinny Woodall and Susannah Constantine. They don't hold back on voicing their self-critical thoughts, but they also show how to love your perceived flaws and turn those unique features into strengths. The book includes a wonderful, thorough section on choosing shades of color that work for you and building a personal palette. They cover details like necklines and sleeve length, and accessories to suit your bone structure and body type. They even go into detail on makeup, underwear, travel, and body changes like pregnancy.

The next step is to go out in the real world and explore! This is not the time to take your entire squad with you because too many opinions coming at you all at once are going to drown out your inner voice. You want to ask some advice from experienced people, and then use your judgment on what looks and feels the best. For example, on someone my size, a three-quarter-length trench coat is going to extend my line better than a full-length trench. The classic trench makes me look like a little girl wearing my mother's clothes. Bear that in mind when you get to the wardrobe lists at the end of the chapter - every piece comes in many different shapes. Take the time to find the shape that's right for you.

High-end department stores like Neiman Marcus, Saks, or Harrods will have personal shoppers and well-trained makeup artists who can add to your knowledge and help you apply the fashion principles to real clothes. You can also sign up for makeup classes at a studio like MAC, or even hire a makeup artist for a consultation. When I was preparing to start pageants, I signed up for several MAC classes on a Groupon in London, so you can even do all this on a very tight budget.

Don't just consult one person. You need at least a second opinion, and you probably want to take the consensus of 2 out of 3 in different places. Even experts aren't infallible. I had a designer friend who tried to put me in a particular design with a peplum and a long skirt. I kept telling him, "No, that's not going to work. That would look great on someone over 5'8", but it just won't translate on me." Eventually, he saw that I was right. It's so important to look at the overall picture and not get fixated on one detail you like.

The downside of exploring in the department store is that the lighting is usually terrible. For some reasons, department stores still have those awful fluorescent strips that magnify your skin flaws, lumps, and bumps. They distort the colors you see and make everybody look like they gained five pounds and hadn't slept all week. Boutiques will generally have very good lighting, so if you can find some with the sort of clothing you're interested in, you'll get a much more accurate look at color.

Learning your personal palette will help you build a versatile, reliable wardrobe and choose the most flattering shades of makeup. There are many systems for finding your best colors. Some of them go by seasons – winter, spring, summer, and fall. Some are named after elements – water, wood, fire, metal, and earth. All of them are variations on warm colors and cool colors and are based on the shades and undertones in your eyes, skin, and hair. You may be interested in a trendy blue eyeshadow, but it's important which shade of blue. There will be at least one that works wonderfully, and I guarantee there will be some that are not your blue.

You also need to have some neutral colors in your wardrobe, but black is not the only neutral! So many women default to wearing black because they think it goes with everything. Some complexions just shouldn't wear black at all, because it is too harsh and adds years or even decades to your face. Dark blue, charcoal gray, brown, beige, white, and even denim can all work as neutrals to pull together many different colors.

For some reason, I especially saw this in the other black pageant contestants – they always wanted to wear black evening wear. But dark complexions radiate in color! So many black women put themselves in dark purple, mauve or burgundy when they could choose colors that are so much more dynamic. Personally, I often have people recommend a dark red or orange, but with my skin tone, it makes me look like I'm about to vomit. On the other hand, light red and coral are some of my most radiant colors. Don't be afraid of strong colors if they suit you. When you're wearing a color that works on you, you won't look conspicuous or tacky, just healthy and alive.

Most of all, enjoy the adventure and hold on to what you learn. Getting to know yourself is an excellent investment in your most crucial long-term relationship!

3. Polish Your Look

Function and form - suit your purpose.

Spending all this time and energy on your outward appearance isn't about being frivolous or wasteful. Doing what you need to do to be your absolute best makes you feel strong to face the world and pursue your purpose. I learned from starting and working with "Dress for Success" that clothing is more than something to wear. We don't just give a woman a dress or skirt – it's a suit of armor. When you are ready to face the day, the job interview, all of the challenges you encounter, you hold your head a little bit higher when you look better. You speak your truth a little bit stronger and clearer when you feel stronger.

I started volunteering for "Dress for Success" some ten years ago because it was one of the only charities whose impact was instantaneous. Sure, we do interview training and on-going support, but the clothes also aid in making a transformation. Seeing a woman turn around in the mirror and having her see herself in a way that she hasn't in years, if ever – it drove home for me the power of fashion and philanthropy and also the power in taking the extra step to feel and be your best.

Suiting your purpose also means making practical choices for your life's work (whether that's a job or a vocation of love). If you work in healthcare or a laboratory, you may have restrictions on wearing fragrance or nail polish. If you're in horticulture or hospitality, you're not going to show up in high-heeled pumps! That doesn't make you any less fabulous. Developing your unique fabulosity is a hands-on endeavor that has to match your real life. You will need to ignore some advice that doesn't fit, even mine.

Essential Wardrobe Pieces:

There are some essential pieces to build a well-curated wardrobe. You should buy the best quality you can find and afford, and leave a little room in the budget to have them properly tailored. These items should fit you to a "T" and be made to last. For most school, work and social scenarios, start with these ten pieces in a coordinated color palette. Adding or replacing these pieces should be the priority for your shopping dollars. You'll get the most versatility if your skirt, slacks, and blazer are neutral. Remember, "Neutral" doesn't just mean "black!" If your work (or job interviews) might require a suit, make sure those three neutral pieces match. Otherwise, tones that look great on you and mix well together are fine.

4. Finish Your Look; You're Worth The Attention

My grandmother is 87 years old and the most fabulous woman I know. I admire her greatly and keep learning from her all the time. She always told me, "Don't ever look the way you feel, unless you're feeling fantastic." She taught me the importance of finishing yourself. No matter what was going on, she took the time to put a little extra polish on herself, and she always exuded dignity and a ladylike demeanor.

We all have good days and bad days, and days we know will get messy. But even if you're having a t-shirt and hat kind of day, you can look like you made some choices before you walked out the door. Grandmother called it "putting yourself together," and it's about being mindful and intentional with yourself.

Putting on some lip gloss and a bracelet or a small pair of earrings may seem frivolous when you're feeling crummy or under a lot of pressure. But that little 30-second gesture sends a powerful message to yourself and other people: "I care about myself. I am prepared to engage with the outside world. I'm worth the effort."

Maintaining your grooming on an ongoing basis can seem tedious or high to maintain, but it's another way to nurture yourself. The right finishing touches can make a $29 dress look like it was $200. It works the other way, too. You can spend a pack of money on designer clothes, but scuffed shoes and gnawed-off nail polish will ruin your look. It's the tiny details that take you from ordinary to polished.

Spending an hour and $40 at the nail salon every week may not fit in with your financial and life goals, but it doesn't have to be that intense. You can keep your nails trimmed and shaped at home for free, and a coat of sheer neutral polish adds a subtle touch of elegance. (Sheer colors also don't show chips and wear as much). It's nice to have fun with nail color sometimes, but if your lifestyle makes it hard to keep up, go clear or sheer.

There are some great quick-dry polishes in the drugstore now that dry in 45 seconds, last two weeks, and come in any color you can imagine or desire. I know, because I use them! I wish I'd had these when my kids were in diapers. I gave up on my nails for a couple of years, because I was changing too many diapers and washing my hands 30 times a day. Forty-five seconds I could handle as a new busy mom.

You may have noticed the pearl studs and string of pearls on my essentials list. They are my go-to finishers for everything from a work suit to a tee shirt and jeans. They don't go with everything, but the things they don't go with are a very short list. Again, they don't have to be rare antique matched pearls or even cultured. You can get a six-pack of simulated pearl earrings from Wal-Mart for under $20 – with real silver posts that won't break your ear out. That's what I mean by being smart about your "fabulous."

As a busy mom, I'm so glad for those makeup classes I took years ago because I perfected my 10-minute face. I don't put on full makeup every day, but I learned what pieces are critical for me, what products and tools to keep ready in my bag, and techniques to put everything on efficiently. Right now I cannot live without under-eye concealer. I may not do lashes or a lot of blush, but that concealer is the difference between looking like I cared and looking like life's gotten the better of me. Knowing I'm just 10 minutes away from full-throttle makes those small steps doable. On days when I do want to be entirely "done," I don't want time to be an obstacle. So invest in makeup classes!

A favorite scent is a wonderful finishing touch. My grandmother always wore White Diamonds, and when I wear my favorite fragrance, I feel like I'm channeling her elegance. I could have on sweats with a tee shirt and a hat, but if I smell good, I feel good. Sometimes people who see my abundant fragrance collection tease me or think it's silly, but I just say, "At least you know when you meet me, I'll smell great."

Regardless of any limitations, you may have on cost, time, or function; you can learn to be self-sufficient and well-polished. Style is a skill set, and you can develop it in a spirit of fun and personal growth. Learning what works for you makes you feel great about yourself, and that pleasure and confidence impacts everyone around you.

The Top Ten:

1. Power Dress: A simple, well-tailored, body-conscious dress around knee length. (AKA the Little Black Dress That Isn't Necessarily Black.)
2. Classic Slacks: A straight leg, not fitted or flared. Pockets should be unobtrusive.
3. Basic Skirt: A simple, straight or body-conscious skirt around knee length or just above the knee depending on your height.
4. Power Jacket: A blazer or suit jacket that coordinates with the pants and skirt. A great choice of color and fabric can make this piece versatile enough to dress up the jeans, or pair with the fun dress.
5. Crisp White Button-up Shirt: Make sure it fits without gapping between the buttons.
6. Fine Gauge Sweater: A pullover to layer over the shirt or under the jacket. Cashmere is ideal.
7. Fun Dress: A softer-cut daytime dress or sundress in a pattern or color.
8. Jeans - dark wash, not jeggings.

9. Trench Coat: Choose a length, color, and style that suits your proportions and skin tone.
10. Upscale Active wear: A washable, breathable jacket and pants that feel like workout clothes, but don't look like Grandma's sweat suit. Cotton Ponte knit pants are available everywhere, in a range of styles from 5-pocket tailoring to heavyweight leggings. There's also a variety of knit jackets that fall between a blazer and a hoodie. Shop around! Get thick material – there is nothing worse than a woman in a lovely outfit with her underwear showing through!

Expand Your Options:

As your fabulosity grows, you'll want to apply the things you've learned to the rest of your wearables. Look for these additional items as you shop (after you've completed your Top Ten, of course!) Stay within your color palette, and you'll naturally find pieces that coordinate with each other. Most importantly – the strategy within your budget.

Tops:

1. The Right Bra: A good-quality, properly fitted bra makes clothes more comfortable, improves your posture, and makes your shape look fantastic. Shop around, set up a proper fitting, and get expert advice.
2. Silky Shell or Camisole: A layer to fill the neckline of a sweater or soften a power suit.
3. Lightweight Cardigan: A refined layering piece for dresses, jeans, or slacks.
4. Basic White Tee: Not underwear! Cut and fit matter here, as does the weight of the fabric. No show-through, please.
5. Upscale Tee: Luxurious fabric, fantastic color, ruffles, interesting necklines or embellishments make a versatile top that can go dressy and still feel like a tee shirt.
6. Silk Blouse: There's no substitute for the drape and glow of silk to add elegance to basic pieces.

7. Nighttime Going-out Dress: Swirly, sparkly, a little daring – whatever makes you feel fantastic.
8. Textured Sweater: Chunky, nubby, boxy, or fluffy, there's a great touchable sweater for every body-type.
9. Casual Jacket: Not active wear. Leather, denim, linen, or a structured sweater.
10. Dressy Winter Coat.

Bottoms:

1. Underwear: Whether you're happier with "less is more" or "more is more," your undergarments should fit perfectly and be in excellent condition. Don't torture yourself with panties that bunch, creep, sag, or leave pinch marks.
2. Opaque tights in your dark neutral.
3. Casual pants: In-between jeans and dress pants. Khakis are a good example, but not the only option.
4. Denim shorts: Life isn't all work and school. Your play clothes deserve attention too.
5. Swishy Skirt: An A-line, bias cut or bell skirt in a fun color or pattern.

Shoes:

1. Ballet flats
2. Sandals
3. Pumps: Neutral dark color to match your Power Pieces, and nude to go with your fun colors.
4. Tall boots: to the knee or over.
5. Ankle booties.
6. Flat canvas tennis shoes: High-tops or low-cut.

Accessories:

The best thing I can invite women to do is start a love affair with accessories. You can keep basic pieces in your wardrobe practically forever, just by changing accessories. It's a budget-friendly way to make an outfit more or less formal and keep it looking up to date. Costume jewelry doesn't have to look cheap or tawdry. Just bear in mind that low-cost accessories have a shorter "expiration date," and let them go when they look chipped or worn.

Jewelry:

1. Stud earrings: Diamond and pearl.
2. A string of pearls.
3. Bracelets: Bangles, cuffs, and charm bracelets.
4. Statement necklace.
5. Statement ring.
6. Watches: Dressy and casual.
7. Brooches – and lots of them!

Everything Else:

1. Classic styled swimsuit: A simple, solid one or two-piece that fits great.
2. Wide leather belt: Choose a dark neutral color that suits your palette.
3. Basic leather purse: Bucket or slouch style to dress up or down, in a dark neutral.
4. Smaller, structured purse: Somewhat dressier. Colored leather, quilted satin, or metallic.
5. Nighttime going-out purse: A snazzy clutch for evening.
6. Sunglasses: A classic style that suits your face shape: Wayfarer, cat's eye, or aviator.
7. Casual tote bag: Canvas or fabric.
8. Scarves: From colored and patterned silk squares to textured infinity scarves, a way to tweak any outfit.
9. Luxury warm scarf: Pashminas in cashmere or fine wool.
10. Signature scent: Smell is psychological. Send a message that you love yourself! (But in a whisper, not a shout.)
11. A splash of trendy. A fun pop of the latest color, texture, or print that fits into your overall style, palette, and budget. Sunglass frames, scarves, watch bands, and costume jewelry are great places to throw in a just-for-the-season item

5

The Terrible Trend Of Big Butts!

Kim Kardashian has one. K. Michelle, Amber Rose, and many others have them now too. Beyoncé and JLo made it cool to embrace our natural posteriors and all of our natural curves. Let's be honest - I have one also. We all do, to one degree or another. Let's face it, butts are necessary. You don't usually see your own rear end, even though it's one of the largest muscles in your body and connects to every move you make. You can't always see it, however, what is physically designed to push you forward can also cause you to be held back and abandon your dreams.

1. "But" Is A Verbal Eraser.

I appreciate the current trend that brings our behinds out front, so to speak, because I've always been on that trend whether I wanted to be or not. The women in my family are just made with a particular stature. I'm sure if I traced my DNA, there's a tribe over in Africa with nothing but Beyonce. I remember when she and J-Lo came on the scene, I dropped to my knees and said, "Yes!" They made it glamorous and desirable to have the kind of shape I was born with, and they weren't going anywhere.

It wasn't always like that. I was teased for years because of the sway in my back, even in middle school. When I was in 7th grade, one of the most popular boys in the class walked behind me imitating a duck. I felt like I couldn't even walk.

My ballet instructor was the first person who made me self-conscious of my derriere and the way it pokes out. She would hit me in the small of my back, trying to make me tuck it under. I walked out of that class saying, "I am never going back there." I loved ballet, but I was convinced it was impossible for me. Believe me, the only way I could "tuck" my pelvis that much would be to break my spine!

I thought my natural posture was wrong and ugly. I felt inferior. Thank goodness for the Alvin Ailey dance company and their truthful vision that non-European bodies could also be beautiful and graceful. Before that, the natural form of our bodies was "incorrect" and needed to be "undone." Now we have Misty Copeland celebrated as a prima ballerina, in all her non-traditional glory.

When I was preparing for my first pageant, my pageant coach had to find a trainer who would work my hamstrings and my glutes in a way that most people don't. They wouldn't let me run. I couldn't even walk on an incline because the more I worked out, the more I looked "wrong."

I never really paid attention to other women's derrieres. Why would I? I never looked at my shape as an asset. I never made a comparison. I never thought about it until this trend. Then I started looking, and realized everybody's behind is made quite differently. There's a spectrum of postures out there.

It wasn't until I was much older that I embraced the essence of my stature, this natural disposition that I didn't have to fight for. The more I work out, the more beautiful it becomes. It's something that people are paying 10 or 15 thousand dollars to create with cosmetic surgery. I see these Instagram photos of people who've been reconstructed and think, "Every woman in my family looks like that!"

Right now the girls who are flat in the back area feel inferior, and like they need to "fix" themselves. Sooner or later, they will become on-trend again. But whether your particular look is on-trend or not, you need to be on-trend for yourself. We all have to embrace what we have. If we let someone talk us out of appreciating the beauty of our natural form, we pay the price in shame, wasted opportunities, and even your health. Now that I have your attention let me put all jokes aside and talk about a real issue. I'm going to show you another powerful force whose influence can be invisible. It can change the course of your life for good or bad and affects every choice you make. I want you to understand the power of words: the ones you hear and the ones you speak, starting with the destructive power of the word "but."

"But" Negates Our Value And Uniqueness.

I grew up for years not embracing, and certainly not celebrating, my natural disposition. It amazes me now how we can allow someone else's words to diminish us. The real sneak-attack on our self-worth is the word "but." People will throw the word ":but" into a conversation with you or about you without realizing they're tossing a bomb. "She's pretty, but..." "She's talented, but..." "You're smart, but..."

Emotionally and psychologically, the word "but" is a verbal eraser. It negates everything you said before that word. When somebody tells you, "I think you're a nice person, but..." what do you suppose they're going to say to you? A compliment? No! They're getting ready to tell you everything that isn't nice about you.

How about, "You're beautiful," or "you're brilliant, but..."? This person may think they're helpful, but they are going to tear you down by pointing out what they perceive to be your flaws. What about, "I'm sorry, but..."? Is that a sincere apology? You know better. They're going to justify what they did and maybe even pretend it was all your fault.

Sometimes we get a big "but" from other people, and sometimes we put it on ourselves. "Well, I want to start my own business, but I don't feel like I know enough." "I think I'm talented at this, but..." It washes away our hopes and desires, and can even negate our dreams.

One of the girls I went to college with had been Miss Tennessee State University. When I was getting ready to do my first "Mrs" pageant, she heard about it. She told one of our sorority sisters, "You know, Juanita's cute and all, but she's not that pretty." She should know, right? After all, she'd done pageants. Who did I think I was?

If I'd listened to that and not done my first Mrs. Indiana pageant, I would never have gone on to be Ms. World International. But I did. She didn't deserve to have power over my goals or my self-esteem. She hadn't earned that right. Had I listened to her give me that limitation, "You're cute, but not that cute," I would have handed over that power to her, and shut myself down.

If we let other people have that kind of power, we can become stagnant, paralyzed in fear. We don't even attempt to rise above the mediocrity of life or pursue those things that we find goal-worthy or dream-worthy. You can't move forward if you're holding on to your "but"– if you're letting those negative words erase everything excellent or hopeful that you say.

Maybe you'll say, "I want to be a doctor someday, but I come from the projects, and my family doesn't have any money." Well, you just erased it! Every time you say that to yourself or other people, that "but" kills a piece of your dream. Maybe today you just erased one letter of that sentence, but if you keep using that verbal eraser, you'll blank out that goal entirely. All you will see is an insurmountable obstacle. You will come to believe the lie.

I believed that my natural posture was not attractive, that I needed to fix myself – to walk a certain way, to tuck my pelvis a certain way. I didn't appreciate myself. I didn't appreciate my silhouette.

I couldn't shake that belief until someone showed me the value of my "asset." Whether it's your physical appearance or whether it's a dream or aspiration, we need to see role models who show us our value and our possibilities. If you have a stirring inside to do something, look for those role models. In the meantime, learn to validate yourself.

"But" Negates Our Dreams And Experiences.

I heard those messages – like from that sorority sister – all my life. "You're cute, but you're not stunning." Now, people ask me, "Why didn't you do pageants when you were younger?" It's simple really - no one told me I was this pretty!

I never thought I was special or saw myself as someone who could be a beauty queen. I make sure I pour it into my daughter, whether she chooses to do anything with it or not. I think we all should feel that way.

Hair was always a big thing in my family and as is typical with many African-American families, as a product of the numerous rapes committed during slavery and the mixed marriages between Native Americans and African Americans, the hair textures and skin tones in my family varied considerably. For me, it was frequently pointed out that my hair was more difficult to deal with because of the tighter curl pattern that I had compared to some in my family. The curlier and kinkier your hair was, the more you were not like the rest of my family. I was always the one with the kinkiest, curliest hair - and it was always an issue. I recall my mother putting a chemical relaxer in my hair at the age of eight – she honestly was doing the best that she knew to do at that time.

Natural hair in the African-American community has come leaps and bounds in the last two decades, but again, when I was younger, my mother didn't know what to do with my hair because it was so different from my sister's hair and different from my mother's hair. They had Halle Berry, and Tracee Ellis Ross' type hair and my hair is similar to Yara Shahidi's curls. It was long and big, and different from the rest of her side of the family - she had no idea how to handle it. Today I am absolutely in love with every strand on my head, but back then we barely had products that were created for the various textures that are presented in African-Americans.

When I was in my first year of law school one of my sorority sisters pressed my hair out and styled it in curls. She turned me around in the mirror, and I saw myself. I said, "Oh, my goodness! I think I might be pretty!" I hadn't seen myself this way before. It was the first time I realized I clean up pretty well. I thought I was cute, but not pretty. There's the "but," that dilution of my value of self and my unique beauty.

Even with experiences and personal goals, so many people let fear box in their lives. "I'd love to travel, but I'm afraid of what might happen." What if it doesn't happen? People will talk themselves out of living. One day you'll turn around and be 65 years old, and never left your state or country.

When I was living in London, people back home were amazed that I'd visited 26 countries. I tried to explain to them; it takes longer to drive from Indianapolis back home to Tennessee than to travel from London to Milan. Travel changes your worldview and changes what your children will see as possible.

I want to be able to look back at my pictures when I'm 80 and say, "You know what? I lived." I think one of the worst things is to see a person in their 50's or 60's facing a midlife crisis because they never stopped periodically to live. You have done the routines of life: bills have to be paid. You gotta do what you gotta do, and yet we all have dreams, desires, and aspirations. If you never even stop to think about pursuing them, your life will be impoverished, and the world will be deprived of the gift you were meant to bring into it.

So I've learned to take the word "but" out of my conversation. I encourage you to do the same. When you let go of the big "buts" that have crept up on you, you can change the trajectory of your whole life – and maybe" other people's, too.

2. Is Your Big "But" Holding You Back?

There will always be these subtle eroding messages out there. If it's not direct from people around us, it's subliminal through media and culture setting these unrealistic Photoshop images of perfection.

Insecurity Opens The Door To Manipulation.

It's no accident that the media bombards us with "but" messages. It's a very purposeful strategy. Whether you're looking at movies, television, social media, magazines, or ads and billboards on the street, they stay in business by selling you things. Before advertisers study photo or design techniques, they study psychology. The whole system is based on manipulating your deepest desires and insecurities so that you feel like you have a big problem and their product is the solution.

The next time you see an ad for a product that appeals to you, really look at what desires it's playing off of. Wanting to fit in and be popular? Wanting to feel beautiful and desirable? Wanting success and wealth? Wanting to have fun and be carefree? Wanting to feel in control of your life when it's out of control? Wanting to be a better person?

Now think about whether buying a product is going to do that for you, or whether it's something you need to deal with inside yourself, or in your relationships. It's entirely fine to buy things you like and can afford. It's not okay to live your life at the mercy of brands and the people who are controlling your mind and emotions.

There's even a whole group of men who call themselves "pick-up artists." They make a game out of getting one-night stands with women, especially women who aren't looking for that type of lifestyle. They have a special term for this "but" talk: "negging." They publish articles and books about how to give backhanded compliments and make women feel insecure, to make them emotionally vulnerable. Disgusting, isn't it?

Let's take it a step further. When someone in your life gives you "but" messages, where are they coming from? What is their agenda? Some people do care about you and are stuck in their limited thinking. They want the best for you. They just have different ideas about what is "best," and can't see your vision because of fear or lack of imagination. You might need to be careful what you share with these folks, but they do have a place in your life, and their caring is genuine. They may have insight into other areas where you can connect positively.

Then there are folks who – consciously or unconsciously – use "negging" to make you vulnerable and sell you their bad ideas. Maybe they are driven to be an authority figure and want to keep you dependent on their approval. Perhaps they see you as competition and want to limit your success and opportunities. Maybe they just want desperately to control everything in their life and your life too – they have a particular idea of how the world is supposed to be and your place in it, and you getting out of that box threatens their little orderly kingdom. Or maybe they're dependent on you and afraid that if you get options, you won't let them use you anymore. Just like the witch in the Disney movie "Tangled," these people create insecurity and use it to manipulate you. They are out to control your mind and emotions for their good, not yours. You have to reject that influence, get that toxicity out of your life, and follow your dreams.

You need to pour time and energy into yourself to replace the things that were erased by all the "buts." You may work for someone else, however always think of yourself as a corporation. What did you do for "You," Incorporated today? You have five or ten minutes today to put some effort into a dream, goal or aspiration. You have it. I've been a busy mom, an attorney, and all those things. You can find it.

What's the worst that can happen? You fail. Or maybe that particular goal doesn't manifest at that time, in that way. At least you don't have to live a life of regret. That's one of my biggest drivers in life: to not live a life of regret. I don't believe in reincarnation. I believe that this is it. It is our one chance to live up to our full potential and your highest calling. As J.K. Rowling said, "It is impossible to live without failing at something unless you live so cautiously that you might have well not have lived at all, in which case you have failed by default."

Don't Let "But" Erase Your Life.

I had a very rough first semester in law school, and when I say "rough," I mean getting low Bs and low C's. You can fail out of law school doing that. If you get too many C's, you're gone – or at least you may as well be gone because your GPA will be too low for you to be marketable upon graduation. It was a hard transition because my undergraduate degree was in accounting. That's a discipline where one plus one always equals two. There are finite rules and clear right and wrong answers.

Law is all about argument and persuasion. It can be very subjective. In law school, you may get the right answer, but there's a better answer. It took me an entire semester to figure that out. I didn't understand what they were talking about. I couldn't get my head around why I was getting C's if my answers were right!

My guidance counselor told me I should go across the street to the business school, get an MBA and never come back to law school. I would never work for a top firm. No judge would ever want me. No company would ever hire me because I had too many C's my first semester. He said, "You are smart, but you should drop out." His "but" negated the "smart," for sure!

People don't even hear their contradictions, sometimes. If I'm so smart, why should I drop out? "You're capable, but you're never going to amount to anything." Well, which one is it? I just remember the color of the carpet on the floor, because I couldn't even look up. I believed him. I seriously considered dropping out.

It so happened I was interning in the tax department at Chubb in New Jersey. My supervisor was Pat Key and the General Counsel at that time was a woman named Joanne Boober. Joanne didn't know me. I was just one of many interns. One day, she pulled me into her office and said, "Juanita, I think I need to tell you that you're great. You're going to make a great attorney. You're going to be amazing someday." I'd been listening to Oprah, and Oprah said it was never appropriate to cry at work. I held it together, but I was shaking. When I left her office, I cried so hard, because I realized this woman was saying things about me that I did not believe about myself. I had let the "buts" erode my vision of my capability. When she said "You're going to be a great attorney," my heart almost stopped beating. After my first semester experience in Law school, I never thought anyone would think that of me, and I certainly didn't think that of myself then.

That conversation and that summer changed the trajectory of my life. That's why I'm so adamant about speaking to girls and young women because you just never know where you're meeting someone on their journey. Every day that summer prior to speaking to her I thought, "Oh well, it's all going to be for nothing. Maybe I can get into the auditing department here because I'm going to drop out of law school." All because I listened to my Law school student advisor – who by the way had never even passed the bar exam at that time.

Some people are so limited in their thinking they can't see any possibilities beyond their checklist. If it doesn't fit, nothing good could ever come of it. I've been a licensed practicing attorney for over 15 years now, and I assure you nobody ever asks about my grades. If it weren't for telling this story, I wouldn't remember myself. I feel sorry for that man now because it must be terrible to be so bad at your job! But I do wonder how many law students just died in that office, over a temporary situation and one person's lack of perspective. It's a shame.

I did go over to the business school and get an MBA. I got my law and business degrees at the same time and graduated with over a 3.0-grade average. I did every single thing that counselor said I wouldn't do. I clerked for one of the most prestigious judges in Memphis, Tennessee. I worked for the top law firm in Tennessee. I worked for Fortune 500 companies: Rolls Royce, Simons Property Group, Eli Lilly UK, and Allegion; and excelled. I even ran my successful practice for a couple of years in the US after we returned from the UK. I was about to forgo all of that by listening to his "but." It nearly erased my future. If I'd quit, it would have impacted my ability to provide for my family, changed my relationships and experiences, and all my future decisions. He almost single-handedly took all that away from me, and I almost let him.

The impact of people's words can be that critical. It could change the trajectory of your life, or it could just cause you to forgo an opportunity or experience that enriches your mind and heart.

When I branched out into acting, nobody got it. Close friends, family, everybody at some point, in their own way, ridiculed me. Until, of course, they saw my pictures on the red carpet at a world premiere, and read about the Best Actress nomination that rolled in shortly after that, and watched the TV show I had a lead role in that aired in the US. Then they couldn't get enough! Anytime you do something that's different from other people, or different for yourself; there's resistance. Even inside, you'll feel an inclination to talk yourself out of it. At first, people will ridicule you and make fun of you. Then they'll ask how you did it. Then they try to copy you. You have to have the boldness to step out and risk being unique. Whether it's accepting yourself physically or accepting your skills and capabilities, you have to start with self-acceptance and stop using that word "but."

3. The Power Of Your Words.

I tell people all the time, I'm not everybody's cup of tea, and the older I get, the more comfortable I become with that. But what I am always, is my cup of tea. I believe God loves me and I'm His cup of tea. You have to be able to embrace the way you were created and the dreams you have.

Even in acting, for every one job you get, you've gotten about 20 "No's." That's a good ratio – 1 in 20 is a good year! But that's a lot of rejection to hear: "You're great, but we're looking for something different." It doesn't matter whether you're trying to be an actress, or whether you're going for a business loan, or getting into school – rejection is a redirection. Don't keep beating your head against a wall, but look for new opportunities and people who are open to your ideas and receptive to what you bring to the table.

Don't waste time trying to convince people who don't believe in your dream as much as you do. I've tried. Trust me; it's not worth it. A diluted supporter is not a supporter at all. You can find your tribe, your team, and your people. And if you don't see them right away, find that level of support within yourself.

Find Your Cheering Squad.

Everybody's not going to see your full potential. The people who do are priceless. We all just want to be seen and understood; valued and appreciated. We need someone who can see us for who we really are. I still have friends that think of me in a limited way. It doesn't matter how many countries I've lived in, leadership roles I've had, how many books I've written, or how many titles I've won. Some people will never see you, and therefore they won't see the things you are called and gifted to do. But the right people at the right time will. The most important thing is that you know and value yourself and that you never lose sight of who you are.

People who belong to your squad are going to see you and your goals realistically and help propel you forward instead of feeding your fears. Maybe you're thinking, "But Juanita, I have some real difficulties here. It's not just my attitude. There is a big gap between where I am and where I want to be, and I have no idea how to cross it, or if it's even possible."

Good. Having concerns is good. If you have big dreams, you will have significant challenges. That's completely different from fear. Changing the word "fear" to "concern" changes the whole dynamicS of the conversation.

You should always operate with wisdom. You have to look clearly at what you're undertaking and make plans to solve difficult situations. In business, we call it a SWOT analysis: Strengths, Weaknesses, Obstacles, and Threats. You've got to count up the cost of time, energy, and resources in every undertaking so that you're not operating blindly. The way you speak about these issues can either help you overcome them, or turn them into walls that hold you back.

Instead of saying, "I want to do ballet, but I'm not tall enough," you might say, "I want to do ballet. I'm concerned about my height. Let's see where I can find opportunities that are a good fit for me." It's a different conversation. Acknowledging concerns is not the same as letting them define you or shape your life.

Look again at Misty Copeland. She didn't start taking ballet until she was 13 years old. Statistically, there was no way on earth she should have ever been able to be successful as a professional ballerina. And look at her body frame – she is lean as she can be, but she's muscular and curvaceous and is not at all built the way "traditional" ballerinas are supposed to be. She epitomizes grace and excellence, and is now a prima ballerina at one of the top classical troupes in the U.S. Can you imagine the "buts" she had to hear along the way? She didn't get where she is without looking at her challenges realistically and working through them. You can do the same.

Now, if you're a well-adjusted person, you know that it's not healthy to have everyone around you just praise everything you do all the time. You can't learn and grow that way. You want people to see you for who you are, and that means understanding your imperfections and weaknesses honestly. True love is accepting someone's whole self, including the flaws and challenging parts. Excellent teaching and mentoring include giving accurate feedback about areas that need improvement.

Destructive criticism tears you down. It makes you feel, not that this one attempt failed, but like you are a failure. It makes you believe you are inadequate and your goal is impossible. It makes you want to quit. That big "but" negates everything good you have going for you, and erases your will to try.

Constructive criticism uses the power of "and." The word literally means adding something more! "And" multiplies your strengths. It creates a connection between your good qualities and the improvement you hope to see. It evokes a vision of what could be. It builds a partnership between the speaker and the hearer. Think about getting these messages from someone you trust or look up to: "You're really smart, and you need to focus on this issue so we can solve it."

"You're a nice person, and I don't think you realize how your behavior affected me."

"I'm sorry, and I want to make sure it doesn't happen again."

Do you feel rejected or accepted? Torn down or built up? Do you feel energized to move forward and grow?

When you meet someone who gives you that type of constructive feedback, hold onto them. This person belongs on your cheer squad!

"And" is also the word of support and encouragement. It turns obstacles back into circumstances, adds fresh ideas for solving problems, and multiplies positive messages about your value to the speaker and the world. When you tell someone your dream, do they give you an "and"?

"That's amazing, and I can't wait to see it!"

"That's a good idea, and I was thinking of doing something similar. Maybe we can buddy up."

"Yes, and I know someone you should talk to who's done that!"

These are definitely people you want on your cheer squad because their support and enthusiasm will help rebuild your efficacy and multiply your impact.

You have to ground yourself in radical acceptance of your natural strengths and gifts and be the visionary of your beauty and accomplishment. Don't allow yourself or other people to speak away the very essence that makes you unique.

Be Someone's Cheering Squad.

As you go through life in your career and relationships, you'll encounter situations where you are the authority figure or the person of influence. Whenever you're in a position of responsibility or a deep relationship, your words are going to matter to someone, whether it's your employees, students, friends, children, spouse, or family members. If someone cares what you think, your words will get hard-wired into their heart and stay with them for years. Use the lessons you've learned in speaking positively to yourself and be careful what you say. Author Peggy O'Mara puts it this way: "The way we talk to our children becomes their inner voice."

Pursuing your purpose and finding your fabulosity is going to grow your life in ways you can't imagine. You may not realize how much someone else looks up to you or listens to your opinion until years later! Be very mindful of how you speak, because you may never know what you're killing. There may be dreams in that person that are just barely taking root. Don't squash them with a big careless *but*.

Even if someone's idea sounds outlandish to you, don't dismiss it or poke holes in it just to prove you know better. Microsoft sounded ridiculous when it was first created. Reality T.V. was an outlandish idea. You may have heard the joke, "Next time you're afraid to share ideas, remember someone once said in a meeting, 'Let's make a film with a tornado full of sharks.'" You may laugh, but eleven million people have watched the *Sharknado* movies. That's a pretty big impact for a silly idea.

If you don't already have people on your side who gets you, it's critical that you seek them out. No one succeeds in a bubble by themselves. There's a very short step from saying, "I don't need anybody else's approval," to saying, "I don't need anybody." But that's a lonely existence.

The journey from dependence to independence is an essential step in your personal growth, but it's not the destination. The goal is interdependence – healthy, hopeful people freely choosing to connect to each other in mutual respect, to help and support each other, and to share their vulnerabilities and their successes. You need to find your tribe, and if you look for it, you will.

The best way to find your tribe is to start being a tribe to someone else. Be the person that infuses value into someone else's life and gives them validation to accept themselves and pursue their dreams. Start today by using the power of your words to create life, vision, and hope for yourself and others.

I can't get rid of my distinctive butt (thank goodness!) I have, however, banished that verbal eraser of "but" from my vocabulary. You can, too. Refuse to negate your good qualities or the beauty of people around you. Instead, evoke the power of "and" to multiply your strengths, create connections with people, infuse the energy of hope, and create a vision of growth for your future and your dreams. Whatever you do, don't forget to give that type of support to others when the opportunity presents.

6

What It Takes To Be Fabulously Successful

Up till now, we've been talking about laying the groundwork and developing yourself as a fabulous individual, poised for great purpose and success. What does it take to go out into the world and accomplish that purpose, achieve that success?

1. Priorities, Goals, Self-management, and Grit.

I've worked with people from all over the world and many different social and economic backgrounds. Everybody faces difficulties and challenges, either in their growing-up or along their road to success. I see people falling into two main groups: those who overcome problems, and those who let problems overwhelm them. The dividing line has nothing to do with your advantages, opportunities, inborn talent, or skill level. It has everything to do with your attitude and your **choices**.

You can spend your time distracted by short-term thinking or overcome by the woe-is-me factor of it all, and your life trajectory will fall short of your potential. Or you can adopt a mindset that looks to the future to guide your decisions in the present, and follow-through on those good choices with purposeful action. Then you will rise.

2. Manage Your Time, Manage Yourself: Show Your Future Self Some Love.

We've done a lot of looking back, especially in Chapters 2 and 4, at how early experiences shape our thinking and how to overcome them. There's a cliché about doing therapy that it's all about healing your "inner child." It's a cliché because it's true - you have to deal with things that impacted your younger self.

When you are ready to move forward, though, you have to think about your future self. Tomorrow, and next month, and five years from now, or ten, or twenty, you will still be you, living the life you built. Who you are today will be your "younger self," and the decisions and actions you take today are going to define the life of that future self.

When I was in law school at 22 or 23, a lot of my friends were focused on partying and having a good time. They were all about enjoying the "now." That's fine, up to a point. But the little decisions I made, and they made - which party to skip, when to stay in and study, who was a good person to spend time with – had a profound impact on our lives by the time we reached 35 and 40.

The average 14 to 16-year-old doesn't grasp why the SAT and the ACT are important. She's usually thinking more about immediate approval from her parents, or acceptance by her peers. And a choice between preparing for a test and getting a good night's sleep, versus hanging out with her friends can have consequences down the line that she may never foresee. One poor decision - unless it's a really major one – probably isn't going to ruin someone's life. But every choice builds a pattern, and the pattern of your choices are the bricks on your path to success. You have the power to make that road rough or smooth, direct or aimless, complete or abandoned halfway.

So as you go through this chapter and the workbook exercises in Chapter 7, talk to your future self. Imagine looking the 35 or 45-year-old you in the eye. She is, in a way, your child. Are you protecting her health? Are you making her smarter, more confident and more skilled? Are you taking actions that will help her flourish? Make no mistake; she will hold you to account someday. She – you – will live with the outcome of everything you do today. Be good to her!

Are you spending the time to plan your long-term life vision? Do you know what your deepest values are? Have you chosen short, medium and long-term objectives that will make that vision and those values come true? If not, don't worry – I'll show you how.

What are you reading? The books and media you consume are the food of your heart and mind. Is it all junk, or are you getting quality nutrition for growth? Making time to read can build you up and expand your opportunities, even when you are exhausted or only have 15 minutes. You can heal and grow your heart by reading books on personal and spiritual development like inspirational biographies, sacred texts or devotionals, or books on emotional issues or improving relationships. You can enhance your education and further your career by reading about personal finance, business advice, strategic thinking, specific work skills, or memoirs of successful people. Plan to incorporate both types of learning into your life on a regular basis. Keep a growth book by your bed to nourish your mind first thing in the morning or last thing at night. Don't forget about audio books. On your drive to work, feed yourself and grow!"

One book to put on that list right away is "Work Clean: The Life-Changing Power of Mise-En-Place to Organize Your Life, Work, and Mind" by Dan Charnas. It's about the practice of "mise-en-place," how top-flight Chefs learn to set up and maintain their kitchen as a kind of meditation or mental discipline. They plan their resources and their time in great detail, but beyond that, they cultivate a mindset that's always focused on, "How can I make tomorrow easier? How much can I prepare and preset, so the next task is as efficient as possible? How can I improve my process to improve my result?" Other industries call it "kaizen" or "six sigma." This kind of thinking will take your personal fabulosity and turn it into fabulous success in your life.

When I was a child, all I wanted to be was a lawyer. That was a big goal, and I achieved it by the time I was 25. Here's the problem. When you have a fixed goal like that, even a big one – what do you do when you reach it? You don't stop living at age 25. You don't stop needing priorities and something to strive for. No one plateaus at the age of 25 – there is indeed more!

Setting goals and learning how to achieve them is not enough. You need a vision for your life. Big goals, intermediate objectives, strategies, and tactics will all fit into that vision and work together to manifest it. Then your life will be integrated into a positive direction, with a strong reason and motivation behind everything you do. Let's define some terms.

Vision encompasses what kind of person you want to be, what values you want to promote, and what kind of world you want to live in. It's your life purpose, and it goes beyond a career or a lifestyle. Vision includes relationships, spiritual or ethical choices, your health and your personal growth. It's the biggest of big pictures about who you are and why you are on this planet.

Goals are specific outcomes or accomplishments. Some people use the word for short-term projects, like training for a 5-K or passing a certain class. Here I'm going to use it for large, long-term desires that build your vision on a scale of five years or more. So a goal might be obtaining a postgraduate degree, launching a significant creative project like a film or book series, establishing a network of supportive friends, or making a career transition.

Objectives are milestones that show concrete progress toward a goal, on a scale of one to five years. Examples might be learning a language, making a significant change in your health and lifestyle, writing a book, or getting out of debt.

Strategies are your plans to get your objective done. Learning a new skill, meeting people in a club or volunteer activity, getting physical or emotional therapy, taking a second job to save money, or investigating career options are strategies.

Tactics are actions and activities that can be done on a daily or weekly timeframe to implement those strategies. Good health habits, delivering your work on time, having a standing date to talk to a friend, and reading for growth are all examples of habitual tactics. Step-by-step tactics might be calling someone to set up an appointment, researching admission requirements for a school, or taking time to do the exercises in the Workbook.

You see how each level and each timeframe rolls up into the vision? That vision is going to set your priorities for how you make decisions and use your time. Keeping an eye on the future gives you a sense of urgency. When you find out, realistically, how long it takes to do a specific action or work a strategy, your timeline for those objectives and goals feels real short, real quick. Having a vision and a strategic plan makes those far-away, abstract goals very immediate and pressing. Urgency is the oxygen to your inner fire. The flame is motivation.

Visualization Sparks Motivation

As adults, we often have to do what is uncomfortable. There are so many times that I've had to have what I call a come-to-Jesus conversation with myself. Obstacles and challenges make you feel frustrated, confused, overwhelmed or just plain exhausted. You can't always feel that inner fire that makes everything seem exciting. To maintain your motivation and keep on track, you have to visualize the outcome you're going for and the reward you'll get from it. Ultimately, nobody is "self-motivated." We're motivated to get a reward of some kind. Self-motivation and self-discipline just describe how skilled you are at remembering and focusing on those rewards in a difficult moment. Those are skills you can build.

Your **motivating factors** are going to be very personal to you. Do some soul-searching and ask yourself the critical questions about who you are and what you want most. There are no right or wrong reasons – just be honest with yourself about your vision, your values, your needs and your desires. I've outlined a series of questions on the Long-Term Planner in the Workbook.

Don't judge your reasons and motivations. You don't have to tell them to everyone because there are a lot of opinions out there about what is a "worthwhile" goal or a "good" reason to work for something. Maybe you want to be famous. I don't see anything wrong with that - just make sure that you're getting famous for something that is consistent with your vision and highest values. There's nothing shallow about being so excellent at something that people talk about it! Use that influence for a more significant purpose.

Here's something I learned from acting: the only motivation that matters is the one that gets you where you need to go. The thing that motivates you is going to change depending on your circumstances, context, and how you feel on that day. I may be able to play a great angry scene by thinking about how my character is sick of dealing with her dysfunctional family. Or if I've been sitting in a makeup chair since 5:30 a.m., that emotional energy may not be there. Maybe thinking about the jerk who was rude to me at the car rental is going to get me there quicker.

A big abstract idea of making the world a better place, may not get you through that midafternoon lull when you just want to watch cat videos on the Internet. Thinking about your paycheck – or impressing the cute guy in your French class – just might. Use what works at the moment.

There were plenty of days I didn't feel like doing my invoices in my legal practice. But my children are my motivators, and if I want them to have a good Christmas that year or take those special vacations, I had better complete those invoices, because they only got paid on the 30th. You need a range of motivators to meet a variety of obstacles because sometimes you need the external why-why on Earth you're doing these things, to go beyond your comfort zone.

Quite frankly, if you develop a decent work ethic and make rational choices most of the time, you can sit in the mediocrity of life and be just fine. You may be considered blessed by comparison to many of your peers. However, if you want to rise above and manifest a bigger vision in the world, you are going to have to draw from somewhere. When you're on task and on your objectives, you may say, "I've done more before 8 a.m. this morning than most people do all day. Now it's 9:00 p.m. I'm tired, I've got two hours that I need to crank out, and I don't feel like doing it." Where do you pull from?

You have to dig deep to sow into yourself and your goals every single day. Understanding who you are and why you're doing what you're doing – and hopefully being able to identify something that's greater than just yourself – will bring that spark to your motivation and see you through.

One thing to bear in mind: goal setting and follow-through aren't just a matter of willpower and emotional investment. They involve specific brain functions called "executive skills" – the ability to "execute" on desired tasks. Executive skills are developmental and can be learned, but they're also partly biological.

If you have a long-term struggle with organizing your time or your stuff, focusing on tasks or completing projects that you truly care about, talk to your doctor. Everything from ADHD to anxiety to thyroid problems or a sleep disorder can make you look "flaky" or "unmotivated." Don't beat yourself up, take care of yourself! Apply some love and attention to those weak spots and watch them transform.

As women, we hear a lot about "work-life balance" as an ideal. I think it's a complete misnomer. I believe you have to focus on priorities and plan around them. If you could get everything in your life to balance out, that means everything in your life is equal to each other. It's not!

I love my work. I have a passion for speaking and writing books. Those aren't my top priorities, and they don't take the first cut of my time. Nothing takes precedence over my children. I schedule my life around my priorities.

This is the best reason I know to pursue success: when you are living your life at the bottom of everybody else's pecking order and just accepting what comes your way, you don't have control of your options, and you can't set your own priorities. You will always wind up in situations where none of your choices are the things you actually want. You're always making do with the best of a bad situation. The minute you surrender to the need to prepare and plan for the future, you are taking back that control. Every time you spend five, ten, thirty minutes investing in your vision and your goals, you are putting your future and your values first. Nobody else will do this for you. Never.

Start today. Get out that Long-Term-Planner worksheet and start figuring out what really matters in your life. Start making a plan of how to make it real. It doesn't have to be perfect in the first draft. The more you grow, the more you will see.

And if you're in a place right now where imagining ten years out is too much to wrap your head around, start at the other end. What can you do today to make tomorrow better? What can you do this week to make next week better? And next month, and next quarter, and so on and so forth. Step by step, day by day, you can visualize, plan, and rise.

3. The Power Of GRIT

Preparation and planning can smooth your path, but at some point, you're going to encounter the unexpected. It may be a hardship or reversal of fortune. It may simply be that your goal is more significant and more difficult than you realized. Whether you're starting a business, buying your first home or just trying to do better in school, you're going to have walls and resistance and setbacks.

Now, you could be one of those people who act surprised that good things in life aren't easy and settles back into comfortable mediocrity. These are people who make decisions according to their feelings. If a project feels exciting, they're all in. But when it feels boring, or confusing, or inconvenient? They're ready to quit. Law schools are so hard on first-year students on purpose, to weed out people who aren't committed. Lots of people think it would be nice to be a lawyer, but it's a demanding profession with a lot of responsibility, and if you don't have a strong reason to do a good job, you don't belong there.

To succeed in life, you need to do things for a good reason. If you've examined your "why" and developed a vision and purpose for your life, then you have a good reason for every decision you make. Either your work is worth doing, or it isn't. If it's not worth doing, why start? And if it is worth doing, then "it got hard" is not a valid reason to give up. So when giving up is not an option, what do you do instead?

You Pull Out Your GRIT.

I came up with this concept when I was working with "Dress for Success" in London because I had to find a way to get this attitude across a cultural barrier. I've observed that there's a big streak of resignation in English society, that the proper response to adversity is just to say "Oh, well," and accept it. When our affiliate was hit with a major betrayal, I could not believe how quick some of the people who were previously supportive were ready to abandon our mission.

I used this concept and created the acronym to rally our group and help them understand what we'd have to do: GRIT stands for Grace, Resilience, Integrity, and Tenacity.

Grace

Grace is all about generosity and support for each other. As a team member, you have to show grace to your partners and give them the same support you'd want to get.

If your child is sick, you rely on your leader and your team to cover you. You have to extend the same grace to them. If you've worked yourself to the point of exhaustion, you need to give yourself the grace to rest before you start making costly mistakes or compromising your health.

As a leader, you have to show grace to your team. We shouldn't enable bad behavior or accept slack work, but we do need to honor our team as human beings and remember that everyone has limits and needs. Sadly, it's often women leaders who have fought hard to achieve a position and become cold and arrogant to the women who work for them. Instead of banding together to be stronger, they let misplaced competitiveness or bitterness poison their whole leadership style.

I once worked in as in-house counsel at a company, for possibly the worst boss of my life. There were three women in the department - the boss, myself and a co-worker, and strangely enough, we were all pregnant at nearly the same time. I was hired to prepare as cover for both their maternity leaves.

My co-worker had a high-risk pregnancy, and by the time she was seven months along she had gestational diabetes yet, she never missed a beat. She was the strongest pregnant woman I knew. Our boss was only three or four months behind her, but instead of showing compassion or honoring the excellent work this woman had always done, the boss became harsh, petty, and downright cruel. She went out of her way to make my co-worker's life more difficult and pile on extra work and stress, far beyond what was necessary.

It got so bad that one day we had an early-morning conference call and my co-worker walked in wearing orthotic shoes because the gestational diabetes was affecting her feet. Our boss turned to me and said, "I'm going to report her to H.R. for dressing inappropriately. Look what she has on."

I thought she had to be kidding, but she was completely serious. Here's this excellent lawyer, a great member of the department, with a high-risk health condition, and this little dictator wants to have her written up for "unprofessionalism" because of her shoes? It was vicious. I'd never seen that level of cruelty in my life.

Don't you know, though, in the last three months of her pregnancy, when the boss became ill and bedridden she wanted all of us to unite and help her with her workload? Who would call me crying out of worry for the health of her child? She understood the value of grace when she needed it, but couldn't find it in herself to give to others. You could also call it karma - what you put out into the world is going to create your reality. It behooves you to be supportive of other women when you can, and when you're in a position of power to never forget the grace you've received, or that you may well need sooner than you think.

Think again of that future self as your child. How would you want your child to be treated by their boss and their team? Indeed, hold people accountable for doing good work, but if you're going to find grace when you need it, you have to put it into the world.

Resilience

Resilience is the ability to bend without breaking. Sometimes you need to be fluid and adapt to changing circumstances. When you are setting out on a long-term goal, the path is never going to look exactly the way you planned it.

That major upheaval at Dress for Success I mentioned? Here's how it went down. A faction on the charity's previous board decided that they didn't want to be a licensed affiliate any longer. They desired to be a British only organization and did not want to be overseen by a US-headquartered company. They decided to break away from the international DFS organization and set up their own, competing group. Without telling the rest of the members, they changed the name on the nonprofit registration. They changed the name on the bank account and retained all of the funds and grants that were given to the charity while it was a licensed affiliate for Dress for Success. They changed the name on the lease and changed the name on the website. Then they sent out communications to supporters and volunteers that they were the same organization, just under a different name – which misled many, including myself, to believe that it was simply a name change but they were still a part of Dress for Success. They essentially stole the charity, all its funds, all the donated clothes, the premises, the sponsors, marketing materials, everything.

Of course, everyone that I encountered asked how this could happen, but charity affiliate agreements aren't like heavy-duty corporate franchise contracts. There were no draconian enforcement provisions and very little that DFS itself could do about it. After all, who steals a charity? It's unheard of.

So here was the rest of the team – including the founder – with no access to the funds, the resources, or even the name. It was a terrible situation, but I knew we could come back from it if the whole re-launch group pulled together.

We still had a mission to accomplish - to empower women struggling with unemployment and equip them to succeed. Our sudden change in circumstances meant we had to change our strategy and tactics. It did not change our goal.

The first thing we had to do was find a new space. We were on a limited budget – after all, we'd just lost our entire bank account – and the cost of London real estate is shocking. For three months that winter - through the snow and the rain – we kept looking for a facility that met our needs. Eventually, I had to go outside the box of our ideal location. I networked to find other options and got creative on using different configurations and kinds of buildings. Eventually, we found a great place without compromising its accessibility and appropriateness, but that could not have happened with a rigid attitude limiting our options.

Flexibility allows you to take a hit and bounce back instead of being flattened.

Integrity

Talent, preparation, and hard work will open doors for you, but it's character that will keep you in the room. I can't emphasize that enough.

Integrity comes from the word "integrated." It means being one whole, solid person, connected and consistent all the way through. When you have character, you are the same person in the dark as you are when people are watching. Spending the time to work out your vision and values will help you make decisions with integrity in every part of your life.

It's possible to fake it for a while – to make promises you can't keep, take credit for other people's work, or pull a little sleight of hand to make it look like you're doing more than you are. But if you're unreliable or unstable in this area, it undermines everything else you're doing. Eventually, you won't be able to cover all the bases and keep all the threads running. A lack of integrity will catch up with you.

Everybody likes to talk about their "hustle." There's even a hashtag about it. People brag about working hard and being clever, keeping their business running on multiple levels.

There's a huge difference between having hustle and being a hustler. As a lawyer, I help people when they get themselves in trouble, and I've had numerous clients think that they can compromise, whether that's being unscrupulous and taking advantage of people, or playing a shell game with someone else's money. You cannot succeed that way, and your business will suffer for it.

Nothing will erode your professional reputation faster than a lack of integrity. A lack of skill or talent, even a work ethic that has room for improvement – all these can be overcome and grown out of. But if people don't trust you, you're done.

I've had to counsel clients before who wanted to sue for defamation or libel – it isn't libel if people are telling the truth about you! The truth is a double-edged sword in the end. It can cut through obstacles and clear a path to success, but if it becomes a weapon against you, it will cut you down. Success means operating with the level of character and integrity so that truth is always on your side.

Tenacity

Tenacity is the ability to hold on, no matter what. The most significant test of tenacity is not just difficulty, but outright rejection.

I certainly experienced my share when I started publishing my books. I set out to do book signings in Ireland, England and eventually back here in America. I had my PR agent and publicist, and we would just call around to bookstores - Barnes and Noble, everywhere. People would hang up in our faces when we made calls to British bookstores. It's no fun, and it's not glamorous, but we kept at it, and eventually, I did book signings in Ireland, London, as well as Lifeway Christian Book Store and Barnes and Noble in the US; and a lot of other places, too.

Remember, don't compare your hard times to someone else's highlight reel. Nobody is going to go on social media and show you a video of how many times someone hung up in their face and told them "No." You only need one "Yes" to move forward, but how do you push past all of the "No's?" You have to anticipate rejection and keep your mind on your motivation.

Everybody that's done something significant has been rejected. Walt Disney was called crazy. Bill Gates who started Microsoft dropped out of college – everybody thought he was mad, too. Maya Angelou never received any notoriety for her poetry or her intelligence until she was 42 years old.

Think about the amount of rejection Oprah Winfrey faced when she wanted to act in "The Color Purple." She wasn't known as an actress, but she was already "the" Oprah Winfrey! After her audition, she called to check in with the casting director, and he attacked her verbally. "How dare you? You don't call me, we call you. We have _real_ actresses auditioning for the part. I don't care who you think you are." Imagine that!

Even if it's based on your own mistakes, you don't have to let hardship get the better of you. Look at Vanessa Williams and her career. She made some mistakes when she was younger, and she received rejection from it and walked through some dark valley days. But for every mountain peak you climb, you started out in a valley.

Whatever it is that you're going to do, rejection is inevitable – but it's not the whole story unless you quit. You aren't going to make every choice or handle every situation perfectly. You just have to hold on and know that there's great stuff coming your way.

It's that same tenacity that got us through the dark days of rebuilding that Dress for Success affiliate in London. It usually takes an affiliate two years from filing for charity status to opening their doors in the UK. Despite having very few sponsors and limited funds; despite digital sabotage and disinformation; despite opposition and hostility from our competitor – I was even personally threatened with a lawsuit – we reopened in just seven months and were able to start serving the women who needed our help.

People left, and right asked me, "Why would you want to do this? Why don't you just give up?" My motivating factor was that I knew London needed "Dress for Success" because I believe so hard in the mission.

I know what it's like to be downsized, and I know the type of support that you need. I thought of all the women we'd helped in the past, and the difference it made in their lives and their families' lives. I thought about all the women who helped me when I needed it the most. And I thought about the women who were missing out on the unique support our organization could provide, free of the kind of bizarre, petty gamesmanship that would undermine our work for the sake of power and control.

They kept me going when I didn't feel like going out in the snow to look at another rental space. They kept me from worrying about frivolous legal issues or becoming overwhelmed with bureaucratic paperwork. I did it for them.

None of us succeed in a bubble. We need help, and we need advice. We find honest people by staying honest. We receive grace by giving grace. Nothing worth doing is easy but focus on your why-why it's worth it – and you will get it done.

7

How To Be Free - The Workbook

Before we get into the hands-on workbook, I want to stop a minute to thank you for walking all this way with me. We have come on quite a journey!

- We learned about the power of Positivity, Preparation, and Purpose.

- We learned about rising above our past mess and manifesting good things in our lives and the world.

- We learned about taking good care of ourselves, right now and for the future, with smart thinking about finances and security.

- We learned about celebrating our one-of-a-kind beauty and finding the best way to polish and present our uniqueness to the world.

- We learned about the power of our words to erase or enhance the good things in our lives.

- And finally, we learned that being fabulously successful takes self-management skills and the magic formula of **GRIT**: Grace, Resilience, Integrity, and Tenacity.

Now it's time to put it all together and put it into practice. This workbook is going to help you build those good habits of self-management we talked about in Chapter Six. It will fill your days with positive, powerful words as we covered in Chapter Five. It will help refine your personal style and develop your Essential Wardrobe from Chapter Four. It's going to help you make those financial plans we discussed in Chapter Three. It's where you'll keep track of your learning and personal growth that we looked at in Chapter Two. And it's the place you'll work out your values and goals - your Purpose - from Chapter One, and stay accountable to it.

I want you to really use this workbook every day: write in it, mark it up, and keep it with you. To make it easier, I'm making available a printable version you can download as well as a separate notebook you can purchase from my website. Just visit iamjuanitaingram.com/shop, and you'll see the link to get your copy.

I want to hear back from you, too! Send me photos of your workbook, your Beauty Adventure, your goals, and all the ways you celebrate your uniqueness at www.iamjuanitaingram.com. Feel free to follow me on Facebook, Snapchat, YouTube, and/or Instagram – just look for @iamjuanitaingram or visit my website. Tag me and use the hashtag #FabulousFaithfulFree! I look forward to seeing your progress and sharing your journey.

How To Use This Planner

The "How to Be FREE" Workbook is based on four sections: Faith, Readiness, Education, and Enjoyment.

Faith is believing in yourself, and in something bigger than yourself. This is where you'll explore your values and goals, really dig down into who you are and what's important to you in life. It's also where you'll plan and keep a reference list of ways to nurture your heart and spirit, books to read for personal growth, and teachers, groups, and activities to heal your hurt places and connect to your larger purpose. You'll spend more time here at the beginning, but it's important to check back and reconnect on a regular basis.

Readiness is all the ways you love on your future self: increasing your vision, planning, identifying resources, taking care of your body and forming healthy relationships. It's got weekly and daily planner pages to keep you on track. Long-term, you'll spend most of your time here, because Readiness powers you through your day.

Education is study, practice, mentoring, and skill-building. Use this section to plan and keep records of your progress, and copy your goals and actions into your daily and weekly planner pages as you go along.

Enjoyment is taking the time to refresh and reward yourself and experience the life you desire in large and small ways. It's important to plan those rewards and keep them in mind because they give you something to look forward to when you're bearing down on your GRIT. Following through on the promises you make to yourself is part of being Faithful and true to yourself. You won't keep "showing up" unless you follow through with those motivational rewards, so make them personal, make them nice, and make sure to really savor them!

To get started, take some time on a weekend or a short break from your regular activities, to have a planning retreat. Sit down and get radically honest with yourself. Make it a nurturing experience! Set yourself up with healthy food, a good night's sleep, plenty of water and some nice tea or coffee. Spend all the time you need to work through these plans, and take breaks whenever you need them.

The questions in the section on Faith are meant to provoke deep thought and reflection. Don't confine yourself to the space on the page if you have more to say! Use a journal or whatever you have handy. Don't feel pressured to get the "right answers." These are for you, not for anybody else. But don't settle for a light, superficial answer. Keep at it, or keep coming back to it, until you feel satisfied that you've struck gold on your core values, desires, and beliefs.

This is a useful exercise to repeat as you progress on your life journey. You are still you, but some of your insights may shift or become more evident over time. As you work through a process of healing and freeing yourself from the past, your understanding and desires will grow, too.

When you finish your Faith questions, move to the goal setting section in Readiness. The same rules apply here - dig deep but don't feel like it has to be "perfect," or permanent. If you still want exactly the same things in 10 years as you do today, you've probably missed out on some growth opportunities in life. But big plans do take a long time to mature. Don't be afraid to start now and commit to a big dream. You will always win just by pursuing it!

Filling out the information in your Financial Self-Care, Beauty Adventure, Wardrobe Inventory, and Polish Plan will take longer than a single retreat session. Make them a priority on your Weekly and Daily planner, and work on them a little at a time.

During your retreat, go ahead and jot down some initial ideas on your Education Planner. You'll undoubtedly add to it over time, but once you've been through the Faith and Readiness sections, you'll have lots of ideas for ways to learn and grow. Don't let them get away.

Finally, indulge yourself and your imagination with your Enjoyment section. Dreaming big is fun! The more work it's going to take to accomplish your goals, the more you should honor that work and sacrifice with appreciation and acknowledgment. The world around you that tries to make you "less than" will also try to minimize your effort and your accomplishment. You can expect to be attacked with guilt and shame from inside and out, every time you celebrate a little win or a significant milestone. Your rewards are your healthy little rebellion against those negative voices.

Choose rewards that are aligned with your values and goals, of course. Make your right-now rewards something that will support your health and financial plans, not undermine them. (Yeah, that means a pint of Ben & Jerry's every time you work out probably isn't a great reward.) This workbook is a whole system, and every part is designed to keep you moving forward in a positive direction.

Oh, and make sure you reward yourself for doing the workbook! Every time you show up for yourself and do your planning, every time you check off a skill mastered, a book read, or a positive habit practiced, give yourself a little celebratory boost.

Your Weekly and Daily Planning Pages are fairly self-explanatory. Once a week, look ahead (and after you've started, take time to look back). Celebrate what went right, learn from what didn't go well, and think about what's ahead. Make notes on your daily agenda about appointments, events, and due dates, but also schedule time for your positive habits, your learning, and your self-development.

Every day, take a few minutes in the morning to be intentional about your choices, and a few minutes in the evening to think through your day. Even if you're struggling with time, money, or personal pressures, this daily oasis of putting your dreams first will refresh and grow your spirit.

Remember, you can always print more Weekly and Daily pages by downloading the file at iamjuanitaingram.com/shop.

The more you use the Workbook, the more real your dreams will become. Believe in the power of these small moments, and they will grow your belief in yourself. I know you can do it because I believe in you already.

And I'm the expert, remember? I have the sparkles to prove it. You.

You are my sparkle, and I can't wait to see you shine.

WORKBOOK

F is for Faith

Finding My Why:

1) Who am I? How do I define myself and my purpose?

2) What experiences and relationships are essential to me in life?

3) What do I value ethically and morally?

4) What do I desire? What rewards motivate me?

5) I feel most secure when...

6) I feel most comfortable when...

7) I feel most proud when...

8) I feel most satisfied when...

I feel most authentic connecting with my values, beliefs, and community by (Fill in the things that are meaningful to you or add your own ideas.)

General:	Specifically:
Meditation	
Prayer	
Group Study	
Formal Worship	
Music	
Video or audio teaching	
Volunteering	
Giving	

Speaking out	
Showing up	
More:	

Books to read for personal & spiritual development:

Title:	Date Started/Finished

R is for Readiness

My Vision - The life I want in 10-15 years:

_____
_____
_____
_____
_____
_____
_____
_____
_____

My Goal - My significant accomplishment in the next 2-5 years:

_____
_____
_____
_____
_____
_____

_____
_____
_____
_____
_____
_____

My Objectives that lead to My Goal:

This year:

_____
_____
_____
_____
_____
_____
_____
_____
_____
_____
_____

In the following six months:

_____
_____
_____
_____
_____
_____
_____
_____

In the following three months:

Strategies to accomplish my objectives:

(Brainstorm and then put a star by the three best)

Tactics:

(Actions I can take in a day or a week that implement my strategies)

_____
_____
_____
_____
_____
_____
_____
_____
_____
_____
_____

Habits:

(Regular daily or weekly actions that support my values, my goals, and my vision.)

_____
_____
_____
_____
_____
_____
_____
_____
_____
_____
_____
_____

READINESS Part 1. Financial Self-Care

My Debt:	My Savings:
Start:	Goal:
Goal: $0.00	Start:

uthentic Confidence looks like...

_____
_____
_____
_____
_____
_____

Authentic Peace will feel like

_____
_____
_____
_____
_____
_____

My Budget Plan:

$_____ per year, which translates to $_____ per month to spend on my Essentials

Wardrobe and Beauty Adventure.

My Savvy Fab Strategies:

(What can you do to be fabulous and frugal? What essential pieces do you need in your wardrobe? What methods you can employ today to make the most of the wardrobe you have and build with pieces that accentuate your best features?)

_____
_____
_____
_____
_____
_____
_____
_____
_____
_____
_____
_____
_____
_____
_____
_____
_____
_____
_____
_____
_____
_____
_____
_____
_____
_____
_____
_____
_____

READINESS Part 2: **My Beauty Adventure**

Negative messages I've heard about my body:	I rewrite them by saying:
1)	
2)	
3)	

A weakness I am sensitive to:	I can apply love by:
	1)
	2)
	3)

My style description:

_____
_____
_____
_____
_____
_____

My color palette:

_____
_____
_____
_____
_____
_____
_____
_____

Fabulous Faithful & Free | 97

READINESS Part 3. Wardrobe Inventory

The Top Ten Must Haves:	Have	Need	Upgrade
1. Power Dress			
2. Classic Slacks			
3. Basic Skirt			
4. Power Jacket			
5. Crisp White Button-up Shirt			
6. Fine Gauge Sweater			
7. Fun Dress			
8. Jeans			
9. Trench Coat			
10. Upscale Active wear			

Expansion Pack:

Tops:	Have	Need	Upgrade
1. The Right Bra			
2. Silky Shell or Camisole			
3. Lightweight Cardigan			
4. Basic White Tee			
5. Upscale Tee			
6. Silk Blouse			
7. Nighttime Going-out Dress			
8. Textured Sweater			
9. Casual Jacket			

10. Dressy Winter Coat.

Bottoms:

1. Good Underwear
2. Opaque Tights
3. Casual pants
4. Denim shorts
5. Swishy Skirt

Shoes:

1. Ballet flats
2. Sandals
3. Pumps
4. Tall boots
5. Ankle booties.
6. Flat canvas tennis shoes

Accessories:

1. Stud earrings: Diamond and pearl.
2. A string of pearls.
3. Bracelets
4. Statement necklace.
5. Statement ring.
6. Watches
7. Classic Styled Swimsuit
8. Wide leather belt
9. Basic leather purse
10. Smaller, structured purse

Fabulous Faithful & Free | 99

11. Nighttime going-out purse
12. Sunglasses
13. Casual tote bag
14. Scarves
15. Luxury warm scarf
16. Signature Scent
17. A splash of trendy

READINESS Part 4. Polish Plan

My style inspiration is...

_____
_____
_____
_____
_____
_____
_____

I get a boost from:

_____
_____
_____
_____
_____
_____
_____

I can make it quick and easy by:

_____
_____
_____

_____
_____
_____
_____

I can kick it up a notch by:

_____
_____
_____
_____
_____
_____
_____
_____

Maintenance "to-do" list - these items need attention:

<u>Shoes-</u>

_____
_____
_____
_____
_____
_____
_____

<u>Jewelry-</u>

_____
_____
_____

_____
_____
_____
_____

Nails-

_____
_____
_____
_____
_____
_____
_____

Hair-

_____
_____
_____
_____
_____
_____
_____

Fragrance-

_____
_____
_____
_____
_____

Mending-

Ironing-

E is for Education

Books to read for my skills, formal education, or career development:

Title:	Date Started/Finished

As you read them, really use the knowledge in them! Make notes in your Daily or Weekly pages of your key takeaways, useful actions, and transformational ideas. Check off each book as you've read it.

Possible Mentors, Consultants and Coaches:

Name/Specialty:	Contact Information:

Now that you've got the information, make sure you follow through on contacting at least one person a month. Keep notes on what you discover.

Skills, certifications, and milestones to master in my education and career growth:

_____
_____
_____
_____
_____
_____
_____

Add these to your planner and take action on them regularly!

E is for Enjoyment!

Right-Now Rewards for showing up for myself:

_____
_____
_____
_____

Ways to refresh on a regular basis - weekly or monthly:

Milestone Rewards for my 3-Month and 6-Month Objectives:

Fabulous Reward for my 2-5 year goal:

_____
_____
_____
_____
_____
_____
_____
_____
_____
_____
_____
_____
_____
_____
_____
_____

The Prize: What is the built-in reward for achieving my Vision? How will I honor my work and my journey?

_____
_____
_____
_____
_____
_____
_____
_____
_____
_____
_____
_____
_____
_____
_____
_____

Weekly Planner

PLAN: I intend to...	ASSESS: How did I do?
Priorities:	Celebrate!
Habits to Practice: M T W Th F Sa Su	Total done:
1)	
2)	
3)	
	Better or worse than last week?
	Ideas to improve?
People to connect with:	Outcome?
1)	
2)	
3)	
	Better or worse than last week?
	Ideas to improve?
Questions to Explore:	Answers?
1)	
2)	
3)	
PLAN: I intend to...	ASSESS: How did I do?
Priorities:	Celebrate!

Habits to Practice: M T W Th F Sa Su	Total done:
1)	
2)	
3)	
	Better or worse than last week?
	Ideas to improve?

People to connect with:	Outcome?
1)	
2)	
3)	
	Better or worse than last week?
	Ideas to improve?

Questions to Explore:	Answers?
1)	
2)	
3)	

Notes:

Daily Pages

Day_____   Date: [/   /20   ]

Morning Journal

Today I am grateful for...	
Today I am inspired by...	
Today I value...	

My Objective:

This week:

_____
_____
_____
_____
_____
_____
_____
_____
_____
_____
_____
_____
_____
_____
_____

Fabulous Faithful & Free | **109**

<u>This month:</u>

<u>This year:</u>

Today I will take action toward these objectives by:

1)

2)

3)

Today I will practice positive habits:

1)

2)

3)

Schedule your actions and habits on your calendar or daily agenda.

Evening Journal

Today I succeeded in...	
Today I learned...	
Tomorrow I can improve on...	

Look ahead to tomorrow's agenda and see if there's anything you need to prepare for.

Tonight I am grateful for...	
Tonight I am inspired by...	
Tonight I value...	

Lightning Source UK Ltd.
Milton Keynes UK
UKHW010638240622
404913UK00001B/83